A MINISTRY OF SHOWING UP

#FORTHEHOPE'S REFLECTIONS FOR JESUS FOLLOWERS
WITH DAY JOBS

ROGER COURVILLE

Help, not hype,
— Roger

DEDICATION

To the men of UGM. Now YOU have a mission.

To Tamar, Maia, and Alden. #NeverGiveUp

To Kelly, Kaelyn, and Colleen Driscoll. Still in my heart.

To Vince. Without whom you'd not be holding this book.

*And to Anonymous, Anonymous, Anonymous, Anonymous, Anonymous, Anonymous, **YOU ARE HERE >> Anonymous <<<**, Anonymous, Anonymous, Anonymous, Anonymous, Anonymous, Anonymous, Anonymous, and Anonymous who make #ForTheHope possible through prayer, provision, and quite literally paying it forward with this book (Matthew 6:3).*

CONTENTS

Foreword v

Are you part of the story? vii

How to read this book. Or not. xi

1. Bring your past 1
   2 Corinthians 1:3-5

2. Holy work 7
   1 Corinthians 7:14a

3. Lunch box 13
   John 3:27-30

4. The greatest story 19
   John 15:13

5. Beautiful glue 23
   2 Corinthians 1:4

6. Back in whack 29
   1 Corinthians 2:1-4

7. AND willing 35
   Micah 7:5-7

8. Crops 43
   2 Timothy 3:10

9. ...all the time? 49
   John 17:23

10. Angels and orphans 53
    Hebrews 13:2

11. Jumping to compassion 59
    Psalm 51:1-4

12. Calling 65
    Ephesians 4:1-2

13. You don't look like a Christian 71
    1 Corinthians 9:19–20

14. Breathing together 75
    Psalm 145:5-7

15. Words   81
    Luke 18:18-19

16. Questions of worship   87
    with William Temple

17. Ramon   93
    Matthew 25:44

18. Boyed cheese sandwiches   97
    John 3:16

19. What to ask an athiest   101
    1 Peter 3:15

20. Plums   107
    James 5:7-8

21. Books   113
    Acts 1:8

22. Soul eyes   119
    1 Samuel 16:7

23. Surely   125
    1 Co 2:10-15

24. Ghosts   135
    Psalm 34:8

    Notes   141

    Book Roger to Speak to your Audience 145

FOREWORD

I've lost track of the number of times that Roger and I have solved the world's problems over breakfast. But I do know it's been over 20 years of mutual encouragement, support, laughter, tears, walking together through life's vagaries and our own foibles. Somewhere between the eggs and bacon (crispy for me) and the pancakes (extra butter slathered for Roger), our bond of friendship has been forged in our mutual passion for words and making connections with Truth -- capital T, for Creator.

Story always plays a big role in our conversations, largely because we both recognize that it is through story that relationships are built. I've only known Roger as a Christ follower, and so don't have any personal experience of his pre-Jesus days. However, the passions he pursued then have been replaced with new passions for connectedness, meaning, and purpose found only in Christ. And while his faith journey I have observed hasn't been a smooth and straight road, it has been a constant, persistent, purposeful seeking, growing, learning.

The stories Roger shares, the insights he gives, the scripture links he chains together, all serve the purpose of helping connect others with the Truth in vibrance, joy, and full color. As you read, may the light of the Good News about Jesus Christ illumine you as you exercise the gift of Showing Up to read, and then Showing Up to be in the lives of those you touch day after day.

John Willsea
November 2021
Portland, Oregon

ARE YOU PART OF THE STORY?

It was twenty years ago, but he remembers the sensation like it was yesterday: the hand on his arm felt rough. But it wasn't rough as in "violent." No, he remembers distinctly that it was rough like it was the hand of... ...of a *carpenter*?!?

The rough hand was the first thing he experienced, but not the last.

The car was now on the shoulder of the highway where he'd pulled over as he reached, literally and figuratively, the end of himself. His face had been buried in his hands, eyes filled with tears, heart screaming out for deliverance from the repeated trips to prison and relapses with drugs.

And now...a rough hand on his arm.

Looking up, there was a figure in the front passenger seat where there had been none before. The figure was wearing something like robes, or a hoodie. More distinctively, there was no face, just a light, and his mind echoed a distant memory... "no one will see my face and live." (Exodus 33:20).

It was Jesus.

And that was his exodus, literally touched by Jesus, healed like the story of the bleeding woman who touched Jesus' robe. Now he's been clean and sober for 20 years.

I believe him, and I believe his story. Because I have my own unexplainable story (see the chapter entitled "Surely").

And all this relates to both you and the theme of this book too, I think.

You see, the man in the story above had people in his life who *showed up*. His parents. His parole officer. And God used *them* in the extended story that led up to a life-changing moment at the side of the road.

For me it was several people...a guy on AOL, another at the office, a couple on the radio.

And I'll bet you probably have your own story. Someone showed up in your life.

But if you've truly put your trust in Jesus, sooner or later you hunger for more — perhaps even wanting to make a difference for Jesus' kingdom.

If so, you're not alone.

Many Jesus followers feel like they are sitting on the bench. Unrecognized. Not in the game. Like somehow it's only church pastors or some overseas missionaries who are "in ministry."

Importantly, "full time ministry" at your job (or anywhere else you are outside of church) *does not* mean is "whipping out the Bible on someone."

I think it's simpler than that.

You *are* part of God's story. Right now. Right where you're at.

I call it "a ministry of showing up."

HOW TO READ THIS BOOK. OR NOT.

WHY

The goal of this book is to move your heart and mind via reflection — to fall more in love with Jesus and the people in his world — around theme of having "a ministry of showing up."

It's not perfect, nor was it even intended to be a book. Here's a little background that'll help you get the most out of it.

WHAT

This book is a collection of podcast scripts…sort of…from #ForTheHope's Sunday Reflection. Monday through Saturday I read through the Bible in a year, and on Sunday deliver something different. Those *reflections*, and this collection of some of them — are about soul searching and story that is consistent with Scripture. Don't expect a systematic theology.

As you might imagine, writing out what you'll say on a podcast isn't the same as writing a book. You need to be aware of how someone will *hear*. Preparing these for written form, then, required choices…how much do I want to try to (re)format for the written medium? (PLEASE, take it from a fellow grammar geek, read for content, not *written* perfection). Too, what about citations and quotes and footnotes and all that…are these *necessary?* Do I want to take out things you'd say specifically for the podcast?

I hope you'll "hear" it as you read, yet also find plenty of footnotes that share sources (giving credit where credit is due), and sometimes even additional thoughts or resources.

HOW

Choose your own adventure. The chapters are arranged to flow reasonably from front to back, but they all stand on their own. See something interesting? Skip around.

Choose your own timing. Read it in one sitting or read a chapter a week? All up to you.

Do it with someone. Each chapter is short, so it would be easy to use over coffee or in a small group to prompt discussion. Feel free to share the digital version of the book — it's free at ForTheHope.org, compliments of those who support the ministry.

Ask questions, share comments. Unlike the many in-person classes I deliver, a book or podcast isn't a conversational medium… unless you intentionally make it so. Feel free to reach out (hello@forthehope.com). Seriously. *And could I ask, purty please, that you share which story or stories you like best?*

Pray. The objective is to fall more in love with Jesus and the people in *his* world. Ask for the Holy Spirit's guidance on how to apply what might bubble up in your heart.

WHAT IF?

What if where you go to work or otherwise spend Monday through Saturday felt more like you were "off the bench and on the field?"

What if your sense of meaning and purpose grew in presence and intensity?

What if the deepest desire of your heart could be rekindled?

Unless I'm seriously mistaken about what the Bible says, we answer those questions best in community: through story and by showing up.

Because when you fall in love — or back in love — everything changes.

Read on.

BRING YOUR PAST

2 CORINTHIANS 1:3-5

IF YOU'VE EVER BEEN TO A CONFERENCE OR TRADE SHOW, IT'S likely this has happened to you: You sit down at a table for a meal with a bunch of strangers and the small talk begins with something like, "Where are you from?"

What we don't often expect, however, is that the conversation will quickly go deep.

Or that God will surprise you.

Hey Hopeful, welcome to #ForTheHope's Sunday Reflection where we pause from our Monday through Saturday reading-through-the-Bible-in-a-year time to consider life and work in a little different way...including what I call "a ministry of showing up."

He'd traveled from south of London, which is a lot closer to where we were in Oxford than me from the northwest corner of the United States. I asked about how he ended up at this particular conference, but rather than the "I heard about it from..." that I expected to hear, he told me his life story. He'd only been a Christian about seven months.

I reciprocated. I shared with him my own story of waywardness, from running from the church I thought I knew with two pastor grandfathers, to descending into a rock band lifestyle (*all* that entailed), to not surrendering to Jesus' lordship until my early thirties. I told him that my own growth had not been an instant, "road-to-Damascus" transformation.

He responded that he'd had a shortened version of the same story, including smoking marijuana.

"And I still struggle with it," he said.

I was floored. I'd just met this guy, and we were already into deep territory that some people never or rarely get to – sharing our respective struggles. I give the Holy Spirit all the credit for what happened next, which was…nothing.

I said nothing.

I just listened.

After a pause, the conversation continued a bit. I don't know if he was waiting for my condemnation or a parental finger wag of a warning. But I had struggled with marijuana once.

Just about the time that we were well down another conversational path, he went back to our point of commonality:

"So what do you think about…weed…?"

The context was clear — the unspoken words after his question were, *"…for Christians?"*

I put my hand on his shoulder.

"This…" I said, pointing back and forth between us to indicate relationship. "…this is what Jesus wants, right? He's right here, right now, right?"

He nodded, and I continued.

"The Bible doesn't say anything about weed, but in the New Testament Jesus talks about wine. He says, 'Don't get drunk, because that's *dissipation*.'"

I have no idea why I remembered that word - dissipation — from whichever version of the Bible that was from. And the truth is Paul wrote it, not Jesus. I completely blew that. I continued:

"…and what he's talking about is focus. He goes on to say something like 'be drunk on me – I want to be in awesome relationship with *you*.' Think about it. If you are in relationship with someone and you get hammered, are you attuned to them, really connecting?"

I was making an assumption, of course, that he'd been in love or experienced the power of connection. He nodded an acknowledgement, and I kept going.

"The Bible doesn't say don't have a beer, it says not to get yourself into a state that hurts relationship, that diffuses your focus, that diminishes that awesome connection. Now can you have a beer and not get drunk?"

He nodded a "yes."

"But what happens when you smoke weed?"

He didn't say anything, but he again acknowledged with another nod. I put my hand on his shoulder again.

"This…" I said again, motioning again to indicate connection. "…this, with Jesus, is the most awesome relationship you will ever have. Jesus wants that with *you*."

And that's where the conversation ended. For the rest of the week the young man and I exchanged hearty greetings and a few pleasantries. He indicated really connecting with something one of the speakers said, and I encouraged him to take it deeper with a book or two. I said goodbye and gave him a hug.

Sadly, I don't know if I'll ever see him again. Gladly, however, what I do know is that I gained a brother.

I don't share any of this for my own self-aggrandizement, but perhaps to share my own amazement. I'm not a new Christian, and now working on theological doctoral degree.

But what God used that day wasn't my elegance or perfect Bible recall (I clearly mixed it up Jesus and Paul).

Instead, as Paul actually did write

> Blessed be the God and Father of our Lord Jesus Christ, the Father of mercies and the God of all comfort. He comforts us in all our affliction, *so that we may be able to comfort those who are in any kind of affliction, through the comfort we ourselves receive from God.* (2 Corinthians 1:3-4, CSB, emphasis mine)

Anytime we see Paul use a "so that," that should tell us to pay attention. What comes after a "so that" is going to deliver the payload of an argument. His argument: Your junk can and will be used by God.

Of course, you've got to, you guessed it, show up.

Why do we numb ourselves with food, sex, TV, wine, or even marijuana? To deaden the pain. To avoid something. To try to feel something…something that ultimately and rightly belongs to our relationship with God.

And why do we fail? Because for a moment we don't trust that He will deliver.

But here's Paul saying that not only will God deliver, but that thing, whatever it is, becomes part of our purpose — so that we can help others.

That's the crazy thing about God. He's never the author of evil, but He uses it. Including the junk in our lives that *we* were the author of.

And if there is one thing that is both unique and beautiful about the Christian life, it is that freedom in Christ produces humility and, dare I say, vulnerability.

This doesn't happen when we're all alone, of course. It's part of your ministry of showing up — not *just* in-person, but with a whole heart. In fact, it might not be in-person at all. You just need to show up from the neck up.

Finally, if you're reading this and *don't* know the freedom and healing Jesus brings, let me direct a final word to you. Vulnerability brings risk. It's probably a main reason we hide behind clothes or cars or Instagram selfies or other trappings of this world. I have been there.

But the perfect grace that comes through accepting Jesus' offered gift changes that. It doesn't mean life instantly becomes perfect, but it does mean you'll experience a peace with your past as well as, dare I say, with every conversation you'll have in the future, too.

You may even find yourself looking forward to your own "ministry of showing up."

IF YOU SHOW UP, GOD WILL USE ALL OF YOU, INCLUDING YOUR PAST.

2

HOLY WORK

1 CORINTHIANS 7:14A

THERE'S A FOUR DOLLAR WORD IN THEOLOGY CALLED "sanctification," and generally speaking it refers to being set apart or made holy or participating in the holiness of Christ. So as you might imagine, the overwhelming majority of writing on this topic is about what we, a people who have put our trust in Jesus, experience. But then there's this curious and unexpected passage in 1 Corinthians about an unbelieving spouse being made holy by a believing spouse. Say what?

Hey Hopeful, welcome to ForTheHope's Sunday Reflection where we pause from our Monday through Saturday reading-through-the-Bible-in-a-year time to consider life and work in a little different way.

And speaking of work, here's the point of today's reflection:

IF there's some form of sanctification that happens to an *unbeliever* by virtue of the presence of a believer, what's the implication here with regard to what happens when you go to work?

Today's going to be a little bit of working out loud with you, but I hope you'll hang with me, because even though we probably will only partially answer that question, I hope I might positively persuade you that you have, as I like to call it, a ministry of showing up.

You might recall that Paul's letter to the church in Corinth (that we call 1 Corinthians) was addressing all kinds of crazy, a big part of which was sexual immorality. And buried in a long passage about marriage is this weird line that says:

> For the unbelieving husband is made
> holy because of his wife, and the
> unbelieving wife is made holy
> because of her husband. (1
> Corinthians 7:14a, ESV)

Your translation may use the word sanctified instead of holy, but that still leaves us with a head scratcher. IF God's work of sanctification is making us holy in his sight after you've put trust in Jesus for the forgiveness of sin, THEN what this passage *cannot* mean is that the unbelieving spouse is *saved* by the believing spouse.

So let's review what we know and figure this out the best we can.

Following Jesus is all about us being transformed into his likeness. It changes how we "walk." John Piper points out that "The reason there is a way of life that fits the gospel is that what happened on the cross of Christ not only cancels the sin (ours) and completes the perfection (his)… that grounds our justification but, in doing that, also unleashes the power of our sanctification.[1]

Jesus had a mission, and now so do we. You've heard me say it before – in the big picture, God is a missional God…it was His idea to send Jesus to seek and save the lost, and it was His idea to continue that work through us.

This isn't just a New Testament thing, though. God's holiness making something else holy is something we see in the Old Testament. Remember how in Exodus, when Moses encountered God in a burning bush, God said, "…take your sandals off your feet, for the place on which you are standing is holy ground."?[2] The *ground* was made holy.

Or remember how, when Paul writes to Timothy, "For everything created by God is good, and nothing is to be rejected if it is received with thanksgiving, for it is made holy by the word of God and prayer" (1 Timothy 4:4-5)? Somehow by our acknowledgement, and perhaps by saying grace or otherwise speaking truth over something like food, it's made holy.

So here's the thing…in the words of New Testament research prof Philip Towner, "The root of this is the idea that things or people are brought within the sphere of God's presence or influence."[3]

This, of course, has a potentially profound implication for us at work:

We don't have to explicitly *share the gospel to move people one notch closer to Jesus.*

Read that again.

I'm not saying they don't ultimately need to hear and believe and repent to be ultimately saved. But there is something to the ministry of showing up. Of speaking truth that's consistent with God's word. Of being someone whom the Holy Spirit uses to restrain sin.

As theologian Wayne Grudem puts it when talking about the Holy Spirit:

"It is significant that the fruit of the Spirit includes many things that build community ("love, joy, peace, patience, kindness, goodness, faithfulness, gentleness, self-control," Galatians 5:22–23), whereas "the works of the flesh" destroy community ("sexual immorality, impurity, sensuality, idolatry, sorcery, enmity, strife, jealousy, fits of anger, rivalries, dissensions, divisions, envy, drunkenness, orgies, and things like these," Galatians 5:19–21).[4]

When we go to work, can we be lovers and community builders by bringing love, joy, peace, kindness, etc.? Yup.

When we go to work, can we influence -- or at least avoid contributing to -- enmity, strife, envy, etc.? Yup.

Can we, in so doing, bring people at work within the sphere of God's presence and influence? (It's a rhetorical question!)

That, my friends, is the point.

I'll wrap things up here by bringing to mind one other thing that Jesus did to turn the world upside down.

In the ancient Hebraic Law, remember all that weird stuff in Leviticus? Like touching blood was something that would make you ceremonially unclean? The clean person who touched the unclean thing became unclean.

But remember the story about the woman with a bleeding problem who was healed when she touched Jesus' robe (Matthew 9, Mark 5, Luke 8)? *Jesus didn't become unclean, but rather she became clean.*

So how does a believing spouse sanctify or make holy an unbelieving one? By bringing them within the sphere of God's presence or influence – in the direction of the good, true, and beautiful.

And how do you do that at work? How do you have a mission in your day job? How you do mission — *co*-mission — with Jesus? How do you bring the good, true, and beautiful to your next meeting? Showing up.

Is it possible that serving Jesus by serving people actually moves them one notch closer to Jesus by your presence, your prayer, your good conduct, and even before you speak? Yup.

But get this: I think it's not just possible, I actually think it's your calling. Your mission. All of a sudden, being a plumber or social worker or software engineer looks a lot less like "just the day job" and is itself a holy endeavor.

SHOWING UP TO YOUR DAY JOB IS A HOLY ENDEAVOR.

3

LUNCH BOX

JOHN 3:27-30

So Charlie Brown's little sister, Sally, is walking along, having a conversation with Linus, and she says, "I would have made a good evangelist."

Linus doesn't say anything, but his eyes widen a bit in surprise. Sally continues: "You know that kid who sits behind me at school? I convinced him that my religion is better than his religion!"

Hey hopeful, welcome to FTH's Sunday reflection where we pause our Mon-Sat, read-the-Bible-in-a-year time together to consider life and work in a little different way.

Better than his religion? "How'd you do that?" Linus inquires.

"I hit him with my lunchbox!"

Here in 2021 you have to be *of* a certain vintage – or a fan of vintage -- to remember Charles Schultz's comic strip Peanuts, but there was a time when it was one of the biggest around, running daily and Sunday for just a few months shy of 50 years.

But I was amused in reflecting about how there was a time not *that* long ago when a comic strip in a public newspaper not only talked about the idea of evangelism, but it assumed that the audience would have enough of an understanding with the idea of evangelism that they'd find the punchline funny. "I hit him with my lunchbox."

Evangelism, as you might imagine, is one of those words that make people bristle. The research shows that increasingly Americans (and especially Millennials and GenZ) believe it's actually wrong – morally wrong – to attempt to convince someone that your religion is correct.

To be fair, there are plenty of things that *should* make us a little sick to our stomach. Some slick dude on TV asking for money. Or like I've actually seen in downtown Portland, a dude sitting on a street corner belting out verses from a King James Bible and holding a sign that said, "God hates fags."

But unlike how the broader culture may be shaped into thinking it's *bad*, the word evangelism comes from a Greek word that means *good* news. That's what the gospel is…good news.

And you've heard me say it before, but it's worth repeating – it's good *news*, not good idea or advice or philosophy. If Jesus is who he says he is, it is good news. The best news. Which makes it a pretty dang good idea, too, but that's not the point. It's news about a person and his work… a person alive yesterday, today, and forever who happens to be the way, truth, and life.

Which means that, if we're kinda in love with him, we should go hit people over the head with our lunchboxes, right? Uh…no.

I'm not here to convince you to talk about evangelism or be and evangelist, per se. Rather, I hope to encourage you to simply consider something we read a couple days ago in John 3.

In case you missed it, some of John the Baptizer's students got into a tiff with a Jew about the nature of purification. The original Greek word in the text for 'tiff' – which was really the word dispute in my translation – is the Greek word is something like "worthless speculation." Anyway at some point the disciples scurry back to John and say, teacher, that *other* dude (meaning Jesus) is baptizing people 'over there,' and some people are going over to him!

John the Baptizer's response:

> "John responded, "No one can receive anything unless it has been given to him from heaven. You yourselves can testify that I said, 'I am not the Messiah, but I've been sent ahead of him.' He who has the bride is the groom. But the groom's friend, who stands by and listens for him, rejoices greatly at the groom's voice. So this joy of mine is complete. *He must increase, but I must decrease.*" (John 3:27–30, CSB, emphasis mine)

He must increase, but I must decrease. The verb tense there is more like 'must continue decreasing.'

The good news of what Jesus has done is profoundly simple. Yet some people don't get it. Even Christians don't get it. Or we forget it. We can't just live by the 11th commandment: "Be nice." Because news includes words and hearing. But neither can we be dipwads about it.

So in the words of Ken Gangel, maybe here's one way we can think about being prepared to give an answer for the hope, the joy beyond understanding, that bubbles up in our hearts when we follow Jesus and begin to even kinda grasp the good news of what he's done for us.

Let Jesus be your spiritual teacher. [1]

Nothing and no one joined the realm of spirit and the realm of dirt and molecules and bodies and car accidents and kisses under the mistletoe and caring for the homeless person down the block like Jesus. Let Jesus be your spiritual teacher.

Show others you're a lover of light.

Not everybody likes that, of course. But then Jesus himself said – badly paraphrased here – people won't hate you, they'll hate me in you. *We* grow up in a world where fitting in is valued, and we got that lesson loud and clear in junior high school. But show others that you're a lover of light.

Never forget your own unworthiness when compared to Jesus.

And that's why the good news is the good news! It's not when we compare ourselves to Ted Bundy, Hitler, or Ghenghis Khan. Or when we devolve into "right christian wrong christian" disputes like the disciples coming to fisticuffs with the Jews. We *aren't* pure enough, in and of ourselves, to enter into Kingdom of Heaven without Jesus and some seriously good news.

And open your mouth.

Proclaim the gospel, at the right time and in the right way. You feed a homeless person because they're hungry. You walk an old lady across the street to keep her safe. But that person in the cubicle next to you? They have an eternal destiny that involves life and death.

Remember, Jesus didn't come to make bad people good, he came to make dead people live. You've literally got a chance to be his instrument servant for saving a life.

May we all grow in courage to love others, because Jesus first loved us.

Or…you could just hit them over the head with your lunchbox.

SHOWING UP IS A CHANCE TO BE A LIFE GUARD.

4

THE GREATEST STORY

JOHN 15:13

THE GREATEST STORY *IS* A LOVE STORY, ONE WHICH WE NOT only can tell, we *do* tell. The only question is, "How well do you tell it?"

In a sense, you already know the greatest story ever told. But do you know how to tell it well? What's the secret ingredient?

Hey Hopeful, Happy Valentine's Day, and welcome to For The Hope's Sunday Reflection where we pause our daily Bible reading to consider our life and work stories in light of God's story. And today, maybe even how to *tell* the greatest story ever told.

So here's how we already know and experience story:

Boy meets girl, they fall in love with each other and a dream. Along the way, though, boy loses his arm in an accident. He can no longer pursue the dream, and girl decides she doesn't like dreamless, one-armed boys.

But that's not how they end in the movies, right?

So he loses the dream, loses the girl, and loses his way, spiraling downward until somewhere near rock bottom he meets a sage who, with some wise words, changes boy's perspective. And before the movie is done, he's figured out he's a fool to think dreams require two arms, she figures out she's a fool to think boys require two arms, and they both figure out that someone who loves you is what really counts.

And if that pattern sounds familiar, it's because not only is the science of story clear about how the brain likes to see stories, Hollywood has figured out how to push our buttons using that pattern. Introduction, conflict, climactic resolution if not rescue, transformation.

Ironically, what academics and marketers and storytellers have come to call that – the "hero's journey" -- just *mimics* the greatest story ever, God's story…but I promised you that it's a story you can tell well, and that there's a secret ingredient.

The central character in The Greatest Story is God, rightfully the sovereign King over his Kingdom, all that he has made. And it's beautiful, all of it, including humanity. In fact, humanity is uniquely beautiful because nothing else in all the created order bears the mark of God -- the image of God – given by Him and imbued with absolute value and ultimate purpose. And *freedom.*

Despite the beauty, humanity is broken morally, a consequence of rebellion against the King…the King who gave and sustains life. Our ultimate design to be in love with the King and enjoy His goodness forever became a course that misses the mark, a course which causes these humans to need rescue. A course from which these humans cannot rescue themselves. A course, cosmic in proportion and needing a rescuer of cosmic proportion.

The Greatest Story's rescuer is both a *who* and a *what*, often referred to as the person and work of Jesus. The person, God's one and only Son who came as the unique God-man to not only live the perfect life that we didn't, but to trade his perfect one for ours – our lives marred with ugly hearts and discord and lies and rebellion against the King. And in the ultimate act of love, he takes our guilt and himself dies a horrific death in our place, offering to trade us that. And when we take him up on the offer – a limited time offer, by trusting the person and work of Jesus, we're born again inside, made new again, "plugged in" to God again.

And The Greatest Story ever told is one where we know the end in advance, because the God who created it all made it a point to tell us. It ends with everyone living forever, good and evil separated, some to the hell that results from God's presence being absent, and some living in the fullness of the joy intended at the beginning of the story.

So how do *you* tell this story? More importantly, what's the secret ingredient?

If you remember nothing else, remember these three words – problem, promise, path. What's the conflict of the current state…the status quo if you don't change course? What's the promise, the desired future outcome, the thing that will be achieved if you do change course? And then how do you get there?

Jesus said, "I am the way, the truth, and the life." He's the path and the promise. And our lives are transformed not because He had a philosophy of some good moral ideas we act upon, but because in the greatest story he gives the holy spirit to those who trust him. God changes you from the inside out – and that's what enables us to be storytellers.

And the secret ingredient?

One witness of Jesus work, death on the cross, and resurrection was a dude named John who put it this way:

> No one has greater love than this: to lay
> down his life for his friends. (John
> 15:13, CSB)

Oooh, does that mean....?

Yes, it does.

The greatest story *is* a love story, one which we not only can tell, we *do* tell. The only question is, "How well do you tell it?"

Because true love may cost you everything.

YOU'RE PART OF THE THE GREATEST (LOVE) STORY NOW.
LEARN TO TELL IT.

P.S. This topic is one of the hands-on workshops I do. See "Book Roger to Speak" at the end of this book.

5

BEAUTIFUL GLUE

2 CORINTHIANS 1:4

THERE IS AN ANCIENT JAPANESE ARTFORM CALLED KINTSUGI. It's the art of repairing broken pottery by mending the areas of breakage with lacquer dusted or mixed with powdered gold.

And yes, if it's immediately obvious where this might go as a metaphor, you're right. But in a sense the answer is no, too, and there's an important distinction that we'll make in today's reflection, The Kintsugi Artist.

Hey Hopeful, welcome to ForTheHope's Sunday Reflection where we pause from our daily Bible reading to consider our life stories in the context of God's story.

The art form of kintsugi is fairly easy to imagine: some beautiful pottery, often a bowl, displays jagged veins of gold gleaming where the broken parts have been rejoined. And, like life, sometimes the finished work is more beautiful than the original…and like life, sometimes little holes remain as a testament to the previous state of brokenness.

But as is common in many ancient art forms, the art form was married to a philosophy. And given that Jesus has a bit to say about how we should engage the world of ideas, let's consider the kintsugi story accordingly.

To start, I just wanted to pronounce "kintsugi" correctly. A quick search on YouTube got me what I needed...*and* a take on the underlying philosophy of kintsugi from Dr. Alexa Altman, a clinical psychologist. She puts it thus:

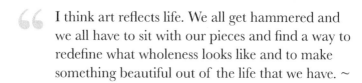

> I think art reflects life. We all get hammered and we all have to sit with our pieces and find a way to redefine what wholeness looks like and to make something beautiful out of the life that we have. ~ Dr. Alexa Altman

She goes on to explain the process philosophically:

- A bowl is covered with cloth, hit with a hammer, and then rejoined with this gold embedded glue. The cloth is like the things that hold us when we're in pieces...a mother's love or faith or inner resilience. She calls it one of the teachers.
- The hammer is another teacher, an instrument of change, whether you do it or it happens to you.
- Another teacher is feeling around, noticing the brokenness, and another is the glue, so on.

I love the analogy, that we're broken but beautiful, that there's a vision for wholeness. And the Bible, of course, speaks to all of that.

One popular verse used in dialogue about suffering and healing is Psalm 34:18:

> The Lord is near the brokenhearted; he

> saves those crushed in spirit. (Psalm
> 34:18, CSB)

Psalms are good for those reminders, right?

But if we keep reading, we happen upon Psalm 51:17 and King David singing,

> My sacrifice, O God, is a broken spirit; a
> broken and contrite heart you, God,
> will not despise (Psalm 51:17, CSB)

Remembering that often in the Bible that "love-hate" language is directional. Jesus doesn't mean you should *actually* hate your parents to love him (Luke 14:26). It's an issue of priority and directional inclination. So to the psalm above, God won't despise, move away from, us bringing Him our contrition. The Hebrew word there, da-ka, is an attitude – penitence or humility. In other words, if you're sorry for doing wrong (versus just trying to escape consequences), he'll *never* leave you hanging.

I had a dear friend once describe her autobiography as swiss cheese…full of holes. And it wasn't until she gave her life fully to Jesus that her heart warmed and the swiss cheese began to be transformed so that those holes were healed. I always loved that analogy.

But look at those verses again. They're revealing in a gospel-shaped way. Who are the players in the story? David, a man after God's own heart, and God, *who David's acknowledging as the healer.* Like maybe David figured out what we need to figure out: unlike the philosophy behind kintsugi, we can't ultimately fix ourselves when it comes to a relationship with God.

There isn't a one of us, of course, that doesn't relate. The Bible has a funny way of rooting us all out, finding us in our hiding places, and shining a light on our stories. Sometimes the brokenness is something that happened to us; sometimes it's us that broke something. And since I'm about to give you a negative example before redeeming the whole thing with one more Scripture verse, I'll tell on myself.

You've heard me muse that I'm a hyper-creative, diagnosed ADHD, and I might be borderline Aspergers. My direction can change quickly, and the good news is that if I'm ever down in the dumps, it's not for long. The bad news is that I can go there quickly, too, and the consequences have sometimes been disastrous choices of words and timing of those words. The complete irony is that one topic I teach in the corporate world is trust, an essential element of which is consistency. People trust what they know. I am not consistent in my very core wiring. I *am* trustworthy, but not in the sense of always being safely predictable.

And this illuminates, I hope, both the beauty and folly of kintsugi as a philosophy. As a philosophy, it seems a lot of sense because the idea of putting your broken pieces back together again is entirely consistent with the narrative that culture tells us. It's so pervasive, we don't even notice it. YOU make YOU. YOU put it all back together.

In his book *Rethink Your Self* (two words), theologian Trevin Wax points out two risks with rethinking your identity in light of Jesus. One is that you turn Jesus into just another inspirational quote. The other is more insidious – that you interpret any cultural talk of "new self" or "new path" as a set of rules.[1]

A new, put-back-together, healed-swiss-cheese identity or story, in the Big Story, though, is what Jesus does in you…and through you. The overflow of a new heart – loving Him and the people in His world – is not self-caused, it's the consequence of the sacrifice of our brokenness given, like David, to God.

And what happens is beautiful. I like the way Paul put it in his second letter to the church in Corinth… he be like 'Yo, God is blessed and worthy…why?'

"He comforts us in all our affliction, so that we may be able to comfort those who are in any kind of affliction, through the comfort we ourselves receive from God." (2 Co 4, CSB)

There IS beauty in kintsugi, seeing the beautiful healing of a mended lifestory, precisely because it's golden at the points of brokenness. And you ARE a kintsugi artist, but not the way the world of art or philosophy or clinical psychology or the people at the office think about it… you're a kintsugi artist because you put your trust in THE kintsugi artist.

THE GOOD NEWS YOU EMBODY ISN'T YOUR PERFECTION, IT'S GOD'S BEAUTIFUL GLUE.

6

BACK IN WHACK

1 CORINTHIANS 2:1-4

DO YOU HAVE, SOMEWHERE IN YOUR FAMILY LORE, SOMETHING you look back on and chuckle?

Sometimes you don't even remember much…the inside joke lives on in a few words, like "back in whack."

It was one of those days long ago when the kids were still young…and my son, the youngest, in some casual conversation we were having said, "Back in whack." Sadly, I have no recollection of what the context was.

But I still love those words!

Now if those words make you scratch your head a bit, trust me, that's exactly what was happening for me.

"Back in whack?" I asked?

"You know," he said, *"like 'out of whack,' but the other way."*

Of course. How could I be so silly? If something can get "out of whack," then surely you must be able to get it "back in whack," right?

But notice something that happened here…for *both* of us.

We both "heard" something based on our pre-existing knowledge. My son had heard "out of whack" and connected the dots to thinking that if something gets out, it must be able to get back in. He did *not* have the context to know that this slang phrase didn't have an opposite…nobody says "back in whack." And because I *did* have the context – or more accurately, up to that moment I had never heard someone say "back in whack." In other words, in a way we each *heard* something based on our view of the world.

View of the world. Worldview. See how I snuck that in there?

A worldview is that set of core, foundational assumptions that shape how we answer just about every other question.

You've probably heard the phrase, "Ideas have consequences," and you may not know that that phrase got popularized by a philosophy book in the 1940s. And today I want to challenge us at the very core with something we read yesterday in 1 Corinthians, add to it something Paul said in 2 Corinthians, and get there by way of something Billy Graham said.

Just in case you don't know, Billy Graham was an evangelist in the last century who spoke to millions. He was actually one of the good ones, the real deal. He wasn't a hardcore theologian, just a simple country kid who genuinely loved Jesus and had a gift for sharing the good news.

Interestingly, as I was researching loneliness I found an article he wrote some decades ago that made some assertions. They're useful, because I think it's safe to assume these about nearly every person you speak to, every person in every culture.

1. Their "basic needs will never be totally met by social improvement or material affluence."

2. "There is an essential "emptiness" in every life without Christ. All humanity keeps crying for something, something they cannot identify."
3. Many, most, or even perhaps all are lonely, and this is ultimately a loneliness for God.
4. They have a sense of guilt, and "This is perhaps the most universal of all human experiences, and it is devastating."[1]
5. And finally, all have a fear of death.

Can you see how these essential drivers play a role in how someone responds to the world? Where they find security? Or meaning? Or community?

I have a friend who's been marching in the protests and riots every night here in Portland. He used to be on fire for God and asking how God would speak into his life. Now his cause – at least what I can see of it publicly – is fighting "the man." Like what Billy Graham identified, he's looking for meaning and purpose, albeit in a place that doesn't last.

You might remember that yesterday in 1 Corinthians we heard Paul talk about wisdom, and he started in by saying:

> When I came to you, brothers and sisters, announcing the mystery of God to you, I did not come with brilliance of speech or wisdom. *I decided to know nothing among you except Jesus Christ and him crucified.* I came to you in weakness, in fear, and in much trembling. *My speech and my preaching were not with persuasive words of wisdom* but with a demonstration of the Spirit's power, so that your

> faith might not be based on human
> wisdom but on God's power. (1
> Corinthians 2:1-4, CSB, emphasis
> mine)

Now does Paul *actually* know nothing? Not even close. He had
been a Pharisee, highly educated. In fact we know that when in
Athens he knew the Athenian culture and customs enough to
quote one of their own poets to them. When he wrote to Titus
he used an idiom of the people of Crete. In other words, he
spoke culture and philosophy to meet people where they were
at. But the goal wasn't overthrowing the system…it was
meeting someone eye to eye so he could then turn their gaze to
Christ and him crucified. He knew what the foundation was.

In fact, in 2 Corinthians 11 we read Paul responding to some
people talking smack about him, and he says, "Yo, if anybody's
got a reason to boast, it's me!" And he proceeds to rattle off a
long list of credentials, but he does so to make this point:

> Therefore, I will most gladly boast all
> the more about my weaknesses, so
> that Christ's power may reside in
> me. So I take pleasure in weaknesses,
> insults, hardships, persecutions, and
> in difficulties, for the sake of Christ.
> For when I am weak, then I am
> strong. (2 Corinthians 12:9-10, CSB

In other words, all of this, and all of me, is subject to the one
thing – the one person – that gives life. The main opponent
Paul was addressing was still seeing the world – and Paul –
through a cultural lens. He saw Paul's physical weakness. He
thought a 'real' apostle would have some special spiritual

revelations. He thought Paul was acting out of self-interest. And how did Paul respond? He wasn't a pushover, for sure. But he says

> Look, I am ready to come to you this
> third time. I will not burden you,
> since I am not seeking what is yours,
> but you. (2 Corinthian 12:14, CSB)

And dare I say, that's exactly what Jesus did.

He came to seek and save the lost (Luke 19:10). He came not seeking what is yours, but *you.*

This week I heard John Stonestreet[2] add a twist to the "ideas have consequences" thought. He said,

 Ideas have consequences; bad ideas have victims.
~John Stonestreet

Whatever people are showing on the outside, on the inside it's pretty safe to assume there's pain, loneliness, fear of death, and guilt. And until they see, in the light of the beauty of Jesus, their need for a savior, they'll be trying to hide, numb themselves, or fill that need with something else. What they are experiencing comes from some idea or belief about something…even if they're experiencing the consequences of bad ideas. We might *hear* someone say "back in whack," but "back in whack" comes from somewhere.

Maybe "back in whack" is not the perfect analogy, but whoever God puts in your path today is coming from somewhere, too. And if Jesus is the way, truth, and life (John 14:6), there's only one way for people to get "back in whack." No matter who they are, they've got *something* that influences how they see the world, something that influences where they try to find meaning or identity or even salvation. Listen for the person behind the words, find what's outta whack, and show them where they can get "back in whack."

SHOWING UP MEANS LISTENING FOR THE PERSON BEHIND THE WORDS.

7

AND WILLING

MICAH 7:5-7

TWO MEN WERE TALKING ABOUT THE SECRET OF A LONG A happy marriage. Said one, *"Our marriage is built on trust and understanding....my wife doesn't trust me, and I don't understand her!*[1]

Hey Hopeful, welcome to #ForTheHope's Sunday Reflection. I hope that made you chuckle because, well, life and love and trust and Jesus and all this can just get weird sometimes. And as I was doing some reflecting and praying this week, I thought about you. Join me on a little journey of thought?

Trust is...a weird thing sometimes. I started wondering what the relationship is between trusting Jesus and trusting people.

When it comes to trusting Jesus, calling him Lord and Savior and following him, I think about something a past friend of mine used to say about her grandmother...that her grandmother would ask anyone within earshot...Are you ready?

I think what she meant, at least in an initial sense if someone said, "Ready for what?", was "Are you ready to die? Are you ready to put your trust in Jesus?"

But then I got an email from a ministry I support and follow who shared something from a book.[2]

Their point: "Not even Jesus found "the ready."

- Jesus called Nathanael......and he lacked openness. Nathaniel wasn't ready.
- Jesus called Philip...and he lacked simplicity. Philip wasn't ready.
- Jesus called Simon, the Zealot...and he lacked non-violence. Simon wasn't ready.
- Jesus called Andrew...and he lacked a sense of risk. Andrew wasn't ready.
- Jesus called Thomas...and he lacked vision. Thomas wasn't ready.
- Jesus called Judas...and he lacked spiritual maturity. Judas was definitely not ready.
- Jesus called Matthew...and he lacked a sense of social sin. Matthew wasn't ready.
- Jesus called Thaddeus...and he lacked commitment. Thaddeus wasn't ready.
- Jesus called James the Lesser...and he lacked awareness. James wasn't ready.
- Jesus called James and John, the "Sons of Thunder"...and they lacked a sense of servanthood. James and John weren't ready.
- Jesus called Peter "the Rock"... yet he lacked courage. Peter wasn't ready.

I like that. It makes me realize that I struggle right along with some great company.

I remember when I got married to the person who is now in the category of "former" spouse. I remember wondering, "But what if...? How do you *know*...?"

You don't.

I wasn't a Christian at the time I married her, and while I didn't choose to end it, it nonetheless did. But if I had been a Christian (or more accurately, had I been actually reading my Bible and trying to live it out) the perspective and wisdom that comes from the One who created us all might have been in view. Even after I became a Christian I failed at really, actually, following Jesus.

Should we trust people? You don't have to look far to find verses like this:

> Do not rely on a friend; don't trust in a
> close companion. Seal your mouth
> from the woman who lies in your
> arms. Micah 7:5, CSB

See? It's right there in the Bible, right?

Keep reading.

Well, how about our feelings, our intuition? Should we trust them? Surely if I'd just been listening to the culture around me I'd have gotten a message that apparently I ignored…to trust my own gut, to trust myself. And then here comes a verse like…

> The heart is more deceitful than
> anything else, and incurable—who
> can understand it? Jeremiah
> 17:9, CSB

Okay, I shouldn't even trust my own heart. And this adds some context to the other verse…because if hearts are deceitful, then friends and spouses and most certainly strangers are afflicted with that disease, too.

So where does that leave me? Where does that leave *us*? So far this all sounds rather dismal and hopeless.

I hope there's a little alarm bell going off in your head. Even if you don't have a ready answer, I hope your spidey sense is telling you that what I've done is lifted a couple verses out of the context of the whole story.

Are both verses true? They sure are…in a way.

Keep reading.

In *East of Eden*, John Steinbeck wrote that we all have one story, and it is the same story: the contest of good and evil within us. *Any honest person knows that they are losing this contest.*[3]

Let's get back to Jesus:

You see, trusting Jesus is about our eternal destiny, but it's more than that, too. It's *continuing* to trust, over and over, day after day, in a way that acknowledges that only He is trustworthy, only He is sovereign and has the power to make it all right one day, and only He will never let you down. Forever should invade your day every day.

Remember those little nuggets about Jesus calling the apostles? The ministry newsletter went on to make this point:

 The point, you see, is that Jesus doesn't call the ready…Jesus calls the *willing*.

And then he promised those same disciples that the world would misunderstand them, even hate them, on account of their following him. He sent them out to be sheep among wolves. He sent them out to wade into people's pain.

Even if what you are doing today isn't "being a missionary," we have the same call on our lives. You actually are a missionary to wherever you show up today. And when you trust Jesus above all else, you can trust people – in the right way -- who you know will actually let you down sometimes.

If we were to read that passage in Micah a little further...

 Do not rely on a friend; don't trust in a close companion. Seal your mouth from the woman who lies in your arms. Surely a son considers his father a fool, a daughter opposes her mother, and a daughter-in-law is against her mother-in-law; a man's enemies are the men of his own household. *But I will look to the LORD; I will wait for the God of my salvation. My God will hear me.* (Micah 7:5-7, CSB, empasis mine)

Ah...forever invades today. God's got your back. He's not calling you to something where he knew it'd be easy or comfortable or safe.

My point is this.

If you only enter into relationship with people you trust, you will always be setting yourself up for a letdown. ALL people walk with a limp. They're not entirely trustworthy.

If you only enter into relationship with people you trust, what you're doing is trusting something that is temporary – their trustworthiness is temporary, and your feelings about it are temporary. It is, dare I say, a fantasy. And this might lead to never entering into relationship with anyone ever (which risks people being seen as transactions instead of relationships).

Hear me correctly here: *I am not saying that we do so with reckless abandon. I'm not saying that you return to someone who abused you. I'm not saying there aren't times when you part company with someone.*

What I *am* saying is pointing that Jesus did *not* say:

- You should only be Facebook friends with people who think like you.
- You should look out for yourself because no one else will.
- Marriage is going to be perfect if only you find your 'soulmate'
- Trusting God above all else means you have license to be stoooopid with extra Os

Quite the opposite. What did he do?

He said something like this:

"Are you ready…and willing? Willing to trust me above all else? Willing to wade into other people's pain even when you know they will hurt you sooner or later? Willing to give this guy or girl a chance even when your last spouse hurt you? Willing to give this guy a chance even though your father wasn't a nice guy? Willing to help that family even though they never say thank you and just take, take, take? Willing to see marriage as a means of making you holy over making you happy? Willing to show up to the leper colony when the risk is that you get leprosy, too? Willing to quit putting your trust in princes and kings or the next election or some Hollywood fantasy or some man-made religion masquerading as a cause? Willing to see that this world is but a shadow and a type of the glory that is to come, *my* glory, *my* kingdom, *my* world where there will be no more sorry, pain, or tears, because I am the sovereign Lord of all creation? Willing to trust me over even your own feelings? Willing to *follow* me?

We chuckle when we hear jokes about husbands and wives – "My wife doesn't trust me...and I don't understand her!" And that's because humor sometimes hits close to home and we know it.

But I hope we also chuckle – in a funny/not funny sort of way -- when we think about how many times we actually operate out of a lack of trusting God. We wait to have children until we have enough money. We wait to start giving until we make enough money. We wait to start serving until we retire or our children leave home and we have time. Oh, and we wait to trust until someone has proven themselves perfectly trustworthy.

Jesus offered an invitation and command: follow me. Seek me first, and everything else will be shown to you.

He doesn't call us to fear, but to courage...in Him above all.

He doesn't call us to comfort, but to trust...in Him above all.

He doesn't call us to love others who are perfectly trustworthy or understandable and have no junk in their lives, but to trust...in Him above all.

He says, "Are you ready...and *willing?*"

SHOWING UP IS ALWAYS IN THE LIVES OF BROKEN PEOPLE. DO IT ANYWAY.

8

CROPS

2 TIMOTHY 3:10

MANY, MANY YEARS AGO WHEN THE KIDS WERE LITTLE, WE figured out that my oldest is an Aspie -- has Asperger Syndrome. One interesting effect of her both brilliant intellect and different way of seeing the world was that she didn't drink soda or pop. It's just bad for you, right? To her it was black and white.

And me? Well, Diet Pepsi is an indulgence.

Nothing could go wrong here, right?

Hey hopeful, welcome to ForTheHope's Sunday Reflection where we pause our Monday-through-Saturday, read-through-the-Bible-in-a-year time to consider life and work in a little different way.

Why do people do stupid things?

My dad's a nutritionist, so I know drinking Diet Pepsi has zero redeeming qualities. It's stupid. But in most cases, it's easy to downplay the things *I* do, AND yet have a lack of patience or even pastoral patience or even Christlike patience with others's stupidities.

This all comes to mind because my bi-vocational job is in my longtime professional field – helping people produce virtual events and/or raise their game with regard to virtual presentation skills.

So yesterday I'm being the producer for an online seminar for a bunch of medical doctors. Obviously these folks made it through med school, so the problem isn't intelligence.

But this one doctor kept complaining about tech not working right, but then would not follow directions I gave her that would have solved her problem. Not once, not twice, three times she didn't, or wouldn't, follow the simple, explicit instructions that would have made her life better in that context. It's a bit ironic, I imagine, because I'd bet she sometimes complains about patients who don't follow directions meant to help them.

And all this made me realize a few things about church and Jesus and, well, us.

As a guy with a pastor's heart, one thing I observe over and over is that simple solutions to people's problems, issues the Bible addresses, but they just won't follow the directions.

To be fair, it's useful to not really think of the Bible as a direction manual, per se, but hang with me here.

It's important to remember that we're saved by grace through faith, not by following the rules...but Jesus also said,

> If you love me, you will keep my
> commandments." John 14:15, CSB

Notice the order of his words here…it's important.

You're not saved by *keeping* the commandments, but it's like Jesus is saying, "a life marked by love of me will begin looking more and more like this, these guidelines and guardrails that I, the Creator of the universe, have shared with you."

Or to add a few thoughts to some of my favorite words of Paul's:

> Therefore, brothers and sisters, in view of the mercies of God, *of all these amazing things I've already done for you – not the least of which was sending my Son to die on a cross that you deserved,* I urge you to present your bodies as a living sacrifice, holy and pleasing to God; this is your true worship. Do not be conformed to this age *as you'll be tempted to continue to do, passively taking the pattern or shape of a mold like Jello does,* but be transformed *in active cooperation with the Holy Spirit* by the renewing of your mind, so that you may discern *and be transformed into the patterns found in* what is the good, pleasing, and perfect will of God. (Romans 12:1-2, CSB, extras mine)

What's the good, pleasing, and perfect will of God? That we'd increasingly be transformed into the image of Christ. If you love him, you'll start to look more like him. And I mean if you really fall in love…like how you want to start spending time together, wanting to please the person you love, and -- to be fair – sometimes *acting* lovingly even when you're not feeling it.

Here's the thing. There are plenty of things in life that are confusing, and to be fair, there are plenty of things in the Bible that aren't immediately clear.

But kinda like knowing, "Yo, Roger!, Diet Pepsi isn't good for you," there are plenty that the Bible IS really clear on — things that are or aren't good for you.

Now the question is, "Whatcha gonna do?"

And that's the question for the people around you doing stupid things, too...*sometimes*.

Some of you know I'm working on my doctorate in spiritual formation, and during class this last summer somebody asked the professor what the secret to being a pastor was.

His answer: curiosity and patience.

And that's it, isn't it? When people around you do stupid things that you know aren't good for them because the Bible's clear that those things aren't good for them, maybe they even keep doing those stupid things, the heart of a pastor is (or should be) shepherding: curiosity and patience.Because what does Jesus do? For each and every one of us? He meets us where we're at, but he's not content to leave us where we're at.

Did you catch that?

In fact, as Paul was mentoring the young pastor Timothy, he wrote

> But I received mercy for this reason, so
>   that in me, the worst of them, Christ
>   Jesus might demonstrate his
>   extraordinary patience as an
>   example to those who would believe

in him for eternal life. (2 Timothy
3:10, CSB)

God's patience with us *should* be its own embodied witness to
others. I was first the recipient. Now I should afford the same
grace of patience and curiosity to others.

Maybe the people around you do stupid things. Drinking Diet
Pepsi is one of them. But sin is also among the stupid things
they do…and the more we understand sin, the more we realize
how stupid it is, how it keeps us from living into all the
goodness and flourishing God wants for us.

But God is patient, and so also should we be. We need it in our
pastors, for sure, but *we* are all ministers of reconciliation (2
Corinthians 5:11-21) who – if we're going to love like Jesus –
need to move from being conformed to the hurried mold of
this world to being transformed into the likeness of his
patience, too.

As long as you don't take away my Diet Pepsi.

YOU'RE NOT SHOWING UP TO BUILD STRUCTURES, YOU'RE
NURTURING CROPS.

9

...ALL THE TIME?

JOHN 17:23

SHE WAS BLACK, NOTICEABLY DECADES OLDER THAN ME, MISSING several teeth.

Me? I was on the road for a speaking engagement.

Like many hotels, the one I was at had an onsite breakfast option. You know the kind – it's not a restaurant, but they have a room where you can get cereal or pastries or coffee. Sometimes they have *real* food.

This particular day I was at the breakfast buffet early, so early that no one else was around. As I was adding stuff to my tray, though, an African American woman walked in.

"Good morning," I said.

She responded with something positive like, *"Isn't it, though?"*

"Aaaay-men!" I said.

At first, I didn't notice *how* she responded. Those of you who know me know that I don't notice visuals like normal people do. I read body language poorly. But I do *hear* communication.

And I heard her voice brighten as she responded:

"God is good, all the time!…" …at which point her voice trailed off in a curiously odd way.

That caught my attention.

I looked up from the breakfast tray I was filling. Our eyes met. As I waited for her to finish her sentence, I must have looked puzzled.

She, though, was waiting on me. I could sense anticipation in the awkward little pause. Finally, she smiled her missing-teeth smile and said, almost like a question, *"…all the time, God is good?"*

Oh yeah. Big "duh" moment for me.

There is a worship song whose refrain is just that, a call-response with those very words: "God is good (all the time), all the time (God is good)." She was waiting for *me* to respond to her "call."

"Yes, He is!" I finally blurted out in answer to her question.

Now she came into full bloom like a spring flower shaking off the cool morning at it strains toward the sun.

"Are you…?" she started to say. She hesitated, presumably cautious because she was on the job.

"Yes, ma'am. I love Jesus," I replied.

At this, two strangers of opposite geographies, genders, colors, and economic statuses had "a moment," a moment beyond words, a moment of, dare I say, *communion*. It was now her turn.

"Amen!" she said emphatically.

If there were ever anything such as a holy hug from across a room, this was it — her beaming missing-tooth smile embracing me and me returning the squeeze with mine.

If there was ever any doubt, in that moment doubt was banished in the lived reality that in Christ there is no male or female, no Jew or Gentile, no rich or poor, no black or white. We were just two people who trust Jesus experiencing what it means to be family, adopted into his family to be His bride, rejoicing and worshiping in a hotel food pantry.

As I and my tray of breakfast exited the food area to look for a table, we parted with unmemorable pleasantries, probably offering each other well-wishes for the day. It didn't matter. In the most unlikely of times and places, I had met one of my sisters.

Some of you will remember that just before Jesus was crucified, He prayed for His disciples *and* all those who believe in Him that we – you and me, Jew and Gentile, white guy and black woman – that we would be one in perfect unity *so that the world would know*...that they'd know that God loves us like he loves his Son...that God launched a rescue mission for us all, offering us the free gift of unmerited grace...that it breaks His heart when any one of us turn him down. (John 17:23)

It grieves me that our world is so divided, but it's also understandable. Because every false worldview deifies something, and if it isn't Jesus that is worshipped, the consequences will only end up ugly.

But for one brief moment, two unlikely people in an unlikely setting got a glimpse of what Jesus wants for us, intends for us, prayed for us. Imagine that...Jesus praying for you!

One day I will see my breakfast sister again, and I'll be ready. I can't wait to be the first to say, "God is good, all the time!"

When you show up for the King, expect to be surprised sometimes.

1 0

ANGELS AND ORPHANS

HEBREWS 13:2

"LISTEN...STRANGE WOMEN LYING IN PONDS DISTRIBUTING SWORDS is no basis for a system of government. Supreme executive power derives from a mandate from the masses, not from some farcical aquatic ceremony."[1]

Aaaand...if you know that quote, it's likely that it evokes something in you, whether it's remembering other scenes from Monty Python's Holy Grail or where you were when you saw it or something.

And if you don't know that quote, well, that's why you should join us as we the Old Testament.

Hey hopeful, welcome to ForTheHope's Sunday Reflection where we pause from our read-through-the-Bible-in-a-year time to contemplate life in a little different way.

A little spoiler alert: that quote has nothing to do with the Old Testament, but... for some of you *the fact that it evokes something is the point.*

There's a curious line in the book of Hebrews, one of those beautiful verses that stands on its own nicely, but if you were there and had seen the movie, it gets a whole lot better.

The line goes like this:

> Don't neglect to show hospitality, for by
> doing this some have welcomed
> angels as guests without knowing it.
> (Hebrews 13:2, CSB)

Ahhh...how nice. It's like playing the dinner party lottery, right? More hospitality, more chance of getting an angel!

Well, there *is* an implication in that verse, a reference or backstory the original readers would probably have recognized, just like some have a memory evoked with a Monty Python quote.

Might we time travel back a couple thousand years to a people who were themselves looking back a couple thousand years?

The writer of the book of Hebrews is writing to Hebrew Christians who'd be situated in a different world *and* who likely had strong familiarity with both the Hebrew scriptures — what we call the Old (or Original!) Testament — and particularly the story being referenced.

The allusion closest to the surface in that whole "entertaining angels unawares" bit would call to remembrance the story in Genesis of Abraham's enthusiastic reception of three heavenly messengers. You remember the one...Abraham's given a promise that nations would be birthed from his loins and his wife...his very old wife...Sarah laughs...and all that. We know how that turned out. (If not, read Genesis 18-19).

But it gets better.

It appears from the text in Genesis 18 that Abraham didn't know the men who showed up were angels, at least at first. Scholars debate this, particularly because some think this was a "theophany" (a pre-incarnate appearance of Jesus). But it doesn't matter...what IS clear is that Abraham invited the dudes to dinner.

So, if you were a first-century Hebrew Christian and had grown up with stories from the Torah in the Hebrew Scriptures, that line from the book Hebrews would have had a little more force. Do *this*, AND you never know...you might get an extra blessing thrown in. So this old-to-us story from 2000 years ago was a story about an old old story 2000 years earlier.

But those old old stories are curious in a another way. Strangers inviting strangers in for dinner? Travelers actual expecting to get invited in to a place to stay?

Interestingly, that was a cultural expectation in the Ancient Near East. You might even recall...

In the NT Jesus relies on the general practice of hospitality in sending out the disciples (Luke 10:7) and in his own travels. As the gospel was spread by traveling missionaries, Christians were commended for entertaining them in their homes.[2] Interestingly, even church leaders are not exempt from this ministry;[3] to do so is grounds for judgment (Matthew 25:43).[4]

And there's even one more layer deep we can go.

Remember how James exhorted that "pure and undefiled religion" is taking care of widows and orphans (James 1:27)? In other words, you're not *just* caring for strangers, you're to show hospitality and generosity to those who aren't in any way in a position to return a favor to you.

Here's a factoid about Mesopotamia:

> The earliest mention of concern for orphans comes from Sumer. Uruinimgina (formerly known as Urukagina), the last king of Lagash (ca. 2351–2342 BC), set forth the first legal reforms in Mesopotamia. *Because of the political situation of warring city-states, the wealthy had been oppressing the poor...*[5] (emphasis mine)

But did that happen? To a degree perhaps. The guidance of the true God, though, changed the game.

We read weird-to-us stuff in Exodus or Leviticus or Deuteronomy and think it barbaric relative to *now*...like it's SO out of touch. But when compared to surrounding cultures at the time, we not only see radical reform relative to those surrounding cultures, but we also see a much bigger picture: a trajectory of God's love transforming the world redemptively.

Widows and orphans and those without a home and strangers, even in the Old Testament, were to be cared for. There was an expectation that they, like everyone else, keep the law of the land (it was, after all, the guidance given by I AM himself). *But there's a heart level issue, too.*

That "heart level issues" is what made Boaz such a beautiful anomaly in the book of Ruth. When he gave Ruth extra scoops of grain already husked, not only did he keep the letter of the law – leaving the corner of his fields for the poor to glean – but the spirit of the law, too.

So what should we do?

> Don't neglect to show hospitality, for by doing this some have welcomed angels as guests without knowing it.

And here's my heart for you.

In just a few days the podcast will be into the book of Revelation, and you'll hear Jesus say,

> Behold, I stand at the door and knock;
>   of any one hears my voice and opens
>   the door, I will come in to him and
>   eat with him, and he with me.
>   (Revelation 3:20, CSB).

The context here indicates that this meal with Jesus, like many of those narrated in the gospels, will be one of repentance and reconciliation.[6]

And it's not wrong to consider Jesus' words as a challenge to our own hearts and sense of hospitality. We should.

But in a beauty unique to Jesus, there is a redemptive arc of God's work visible through history, a reminder that the same God who has kept all his promises will keep those which for us are in history that hasn't happened yet.

Best of all, it speaks to every human heart that longs to belong. To have a home. To know and be known. You have a chance to give a gift when you open your doors to widows and orphans and neighbors and strangers and podcast host ministers, you never know, angels or even Jesus.

HOSPITALITY IS FIRST AND BEST A SHOWING UP OF THE HEART.

JUMPING TO COMPASSION

PSALM 51:1-4

THE PLANE — WITH ME IN IT — LANDED IN HOUSTON, TEXAS. And I was anxious to get off.

I knew I had a ride waiting for me, a ride that was going to take me straight to an important dinner with the board members of an association that had hired me to speak the next day. I'd felt lucky, too as I was able to book a seat that was forward in the plane. Time was going to be tight for getting to the dinner on time, and spending less time deboarding from the front of the plane would save precious minutes.

But then…

When it was my "turn" to step into the aisle, a young guy cuts right in front of me with a lurch. There was no "I need to make a connecting flight", not even eye contact that communicated something.

"Whatever," I thought. "Clearly this dingleberry thinks his time schedule is more important than mine. How presumptuous."

My thoughts didn't get kinder from there.

This guy then begins an epic struggle, one he was mostly losing, trying to dislodge a bag from the overhead bin, and traffic starts backing up behind us.

While waiting I was head-down, partly to change up the music playlist that was ringing in my ears and partly because I had time to check email and social media (and both of these while drawing ever more impatient).

When we did start moving, you could barely call it moving. It was more one of those moving-not-moving kinds of slowness that didn't require me to even raise my gaze. We shuffled forward. Barely.

As we left the plane and started up the ramp to the terminal I shifted gears. It was time to blow past this driver...but this idiot was driving in both lanes! Walking smack in the middle of the ramp in a way that continued to block me and everyone behind me from passing! Definitely inconsiderate! More unkind thoughts! And then...

I raised my gaze.

Bam!

It hit me and, well...

I noticed he was limping.

This was not just a "my foot hurts" kind of limp. This was a deformity-or-birth-defect kind of limp.

I had kinda kept my peripheral vision on his upper body. I didn't pay more attention because I didn't need to — we'd been going nowhere fast. And his upper body was upright and steady. But down below his lower body swayed and contorted, accommodating his handicap so as to keep that upper part upright and steady as he walked along.

"Oh God," I murmured in silent prayer, "forgive me for jumping to…"

"…*compassion?*" God replied. And he kept talking:

"You jumped right to compassion, didn't you? You gave him the benefit of the doubt, right? Because, after all, you know that even if you don't see someone limp, every single person you meet has something going on in their lives that needs your understanding, right? You immediately jumped to compassion because this guy is someone that I love and made in MY image, right? And you started from a place of love and compassion just like I taught you, right?"

I was silent.

I turned off the music.

My low-hanging head was now hanging in shame.

For our Sunday reflection today this got me thinking about an Old Testament story, a story of a King. King David's story was a beloved rags-to-riches story of a shepherd boy turned hero warrior and gifted poet, a real Renaissance guy some 2600 years before the Renaissance.

Except that he lost his way, too.

You remember the story. David fell into lust with a woman named Bathsheba, beds her, gets her pregnant, and *then* tries to cover it up by making sure her husband – an honorable guy, no less – got killed in battle.

The whole plot went down in flames, of course, and it took the prophet Nathan calling David out on his junk to bring him to his knees in repentance. (see 2 Samuel 11-12)

Like any good songwriter, David didn't let the pain go to waste. Here he is, guilty of both adultery and murder (both capital offenses in ancient Jewish law!), and how does he respond?

The song we now read as Psalm 51 begins this way:

> Be gracious to me, God,
> according to your faithful love;
> according to your abundant compassion,
> blot out my rebellion.
> Completely wash away my guilt
> and cleanse me from my sin.
> For I am conscious of my rebellion,
> and my sin is always before me.
> Against you—you alone—I have sinned
> and done this evil in your sight.
> So you are right when you pass
> sentence;
> you are blameless when you judge.
> (Psalm 51:1-4, CSB)

I imagine David, the greatest of all the earthly Israelite kings, laying prostrate on the ground in a show of complete humility and humiliation. And yet this is the same David that God Himself spoke about through the prophet Samuel, calling him "a man after God's own heart" (1 Samuel 13:14). Why? Because of his awesomeness? No, because he acknowledged his brokenness before the only One who could save him from himself.

The good news, my friends, is that there is no one beyond the reach of God's lovingkindness. Not David, not me, not you. Realizing this, David's sings a song of remorse that he has *ultimately* wronged someone who loves him more than is imaginable – not just Bathsheba and Uriah, but his perfectly good Creator. He knows what he deserves. And you can hear his heart breaking as he sings the first line, "Be gracious to me, God."

The reminder in this story of David is that all are broken, all are welcome, and all are called to repentance. No one's sin is exempt, but grace is available to each and every person...

- ...even for those who abuse their power.
- ...even for those whose pride keeps them from acknowledging their need.
- ...even for those whose pain keeps them drinking at the well of self-medication.
- ...even for those who think they're off the hook because "it was just a little white lie." Or "just a little bit of gossiping behind someone's back, but it was *true!*"
- ...even for those whose secret sin isn't known by anyone else.

And even for a guy on an airplane jumping to conclusions about another guy who cut him off in the airplane aisle.

This guy had stumbled in front of me because it was, in fact, a stumble. And maybe he sensed every word I *didn't* say. I don't know.

But God did. And it was like I could hear God's heart break at my failure. I could hear Him asking me, gently, "Did you jump to compassion or jump to conclusion?"

"Guilty as charged," I whispered under my breath. "I most definitely did NOT jump to compassion. Be gracious to me, O God."

And then came his reply: "I love you, Roger. Now go and do likewise."

GOD ISN'T COUNTING ON YOUR PERFECTION, HE WANTS TO HELP YOU SHOW UP WITH YOUR FAITHFULNESS.

CALLING

EPHESIANS 4:1-2

So there we were, roadtripping through the Rocky Mountains and camping along the way, the trip taking us to Grand Teton National Park and Yellowstone in Wyoming, and eventually to Glacier National Park in Montana. In fact, it's from Yellowstone *to* Glacier that we crossed the border from Wyoming into Montana…and then saw a sign welcoming us back to Wyoming? What? We had *not* turned around.

Hey hopeful, welcome to #ForTheHope's Sunday Reflection where we pause from our read-through-the-Bible-in-a-year time to contemplate life in a little different way.

But back to this weirdness in Montana. Or was it Wyoming?

You see, my roadtrip buddy and I headed out of Yellowstone, not really paying attention very well. Seeing the state line for Montana made sense…we were on our way to Glacier National Park, after all. But since we'd not reversed course, seeing a sign welcoming us back to Wyoming made no sense at all.

And you might have guessed it – if you leave Yellowstone going *east* instead of *north*, you do in fact end up on a road that tilts up into Montana …and back into Wyoming again.

There is a limit to analogies, and particularly this one. But as it regards calling, it kicks us off pretty well. You see, it's pretty common – and I've done this myself – to wish God would just make your life calling really clear. After all, he reached out and gave Moses and Abraham and Saul of Tarsus unmistakable kicks in their backsides, right?

As it turns out, he *has* made clear the calling of every human being. Many extraordinary stories are descriptive, not prescriptive. And it's God's prerogative to do things that appear to us to be unique and miraculous. Not that what I'm about to share isn't miraculous, but in a different way.

So here we headed to Montana, and this is what it's like when you're lost. You're on a path. Except that before you figure out you're lost, *you're lost and don't know it yet.* We had no idea we'd made a colossal mistake until we saw – from Montana – the sign saying welome to Wyoming. And even then we're like, "Uh, whuht?"

Recognizing our own lostness is actually the first part of the "calling" on every human being. Theologians call it "general revelation" — the idea that we can know (just from live in the cosmos) that there's a moral law and that we don't measure up. Sooner or later we figure out we're lost (Romans 1:19).

As my buddy and I continued on the road trip, we found a place to camp…but it wasn't very long before we saw some dark clouds gathering. We hadn't even gotten the tents set up yet, and we were looking forward to a fire and hot meal, but spending the night in a tent in the rain sounded like no fun at all…so we packed up and decided to keep driving.

Ironically, continuing along the same road in the same direction came to a series of switchback up the steep side of the Rocky Mountains…and as we climbed in elevation, we could look back down over a valley to the west..and the most spectacular sunset I'd ever seen. Moreover, as the sun went down and long shadows crept across the valley floor toward us, we kept climbing – so it lengthened the amount of time we were catching the sun just at the right angle. And a 15 minute sunset stretched into a 45 minute sunset.

You've probably heard the phrase, "Give up to go up" or "Give up to grow up." But therein lies a second calling, too – that we're called to be transformed. Notice two things:

One, there is a cost to change. Jesus made it clear that following him would come with a cost. It's Jesus who, as part of God's overall mission to humanity, said "For the Son of Man has come to seek and to save the lost" (Luke 19:10, CSB). The next part of the call on every human is his: "Follow me." But that means turning *from* something *to* something else (him). What Jesus didn't say is exactly what we'd experience along the way.

If my roadtrip buddy and I hadn't gotten back on the road, we'd have missed the most spectacular and longest sunset of our lives.

The second thing to notice, though, is an order of things." Transformation that comes from following Jesus comes as a result of action – it's not action to result. We don't save ourselves. We don't "do this so we can get to God," we receive the free gift offered and then as we follow, transformation happens. It was a set of storm clouds that got us off our duffs on the roadtrip…and in our lives, often times something happens that makes us realize we're lost and in need of a savior.

Remember how Paul wrote this to the church in Ephesus:

> I therefore, a prisoner for the Lord, urge
>   you to walk in a manner worthy of
>   the calling to which you have been
>   called, with all humility and
>   gentleness, with patience, bearing
>   with one another in love, eager to
>   maintain the unity of the Spirit in
>   the bond of peace. (Ephesians
>   4:1-3, CSB)

Did you catch that word "bearing?" Bearing with one another? Paul just described *work*…work as it relates to *relationship*. That's "bearing" like "put up with" or "endure." Because while I know I'm perfect, I know you aren't, and I *guess* I'll be patient with bear with *you*. Yeah, wrong attitude.

After you respond to the calling to follow, you're then called to be transformed.

And that new identity in Christ, that transformation – at least according to the Bible -- is something that happens in the context of relationship. We're not made to grow on our own, and we're not made even to understand our identities on our own. No, we're to do it via a third aspect of calling – serving others.

When Paul was kicking off his letter to the church in Rome he wrote:

> For I want very much to see you, so that
>   I may impart to you some spiritual
>   gift to strengthen you, that is, to be
>   mutually encouraged by each other's

> faith, both yours and mine. (Romans
> 1:11–12, CSB)

Now this isn't the only verse that goes here, but I chose this one because it shows mutuality. Paul doesn't get to use his gifts if he's not with them, and they don't get to use their gifts with him. Oh, kinda like you've got to *show up*, right?

Remember, way back in Genesis God made it clear his own mission was for all people: "Yo Abraham, I choose you, and here's what you're going to experience, but I'm going to reach the whole world with and through you" (Genesis 22, Roger Paraphrased Version)

Why did God do it this way? I don't know. And we know stories of, say, a Muslim coming to Christ via a dream – but those are exceptions, not the rule. Just like the spectacular callings in the Bible are the exceptions, not the rule. And besides, we're not talking about all people right now, per se, we're talking about you. Abraham had a choice and could have said no. And so could you.

Jesus is calling saying "follow me." You don't know where that goes, but that's not the issue on the table.

The issue is one of trusting him for salvation from death and for life. And then he says, "follow me." And you still don't know exactly where that will go, but most of you will follow me while you're plumbers or teachers or social workers or software engineers or food truck entrepreneurs. There will be a cost, but there will also be the reward of an increasing sense of shalom (peace).

By the way, shalom isn't just for you. It's a ministry of showing up. It's actually a calling to full time ministry – right where you're at Monday through Friday – showing up as a temple of the Holy Spirit, participating in the Holy Spirit's mission in the world, and with an assignment and gifting that's probably different than mine. But if you don't show up, you're not in position to serve someone else by using the gifts God has given uniquely.

I told you the roadtrip to Montana was an imperfect analogy. There was no part of it that involved serving others, and I wasn't a Jesus follower at the time anyway.

But when we're lost we're called to follow. When we follow we're called to intentionally grow. And the way we intentionally grow is by serving others.

And the good news is that saying "here I am" when Jesus says, "follow me" is the path your heart longs for, joyous on the way, and ultimately leading home.

Zig Ziglar once said,

 You will get all you want in life if you help enough other people get what they want.

It's kinda like he was reading the Bible and talking about "calling."

Go figure.

WE GROW OURSELVES IN LIGHT OF SHOWING UP TO SERVE OTHERS.

13

YOU DON'T LOOK LIKE A CHRISTIAN

1 CORINTHIANS 9:19–20

"YOU'RE A CHRISTIAN? YOU DON'T LOOK LIKE A CHRISTIAN."

"And just what does a Christian look like?" I asked.

Her not-real name is Julie, and I'd just bumped into her at the grocery store I frequent. Most of the time our interactions were short because she was behind a register. And that meant all I knew about her was her first name.

But this time was different.

Hey hopeful, welcome to the FTH's Sunday Reflection where we pause from our Mon-Sat, read-through-the-Bible-in-a-year time and consider our life and work stories in light of God's story.

Back to Julie. This time around Julie and I exchanged the typical pleasantries, but this time there was no one around. I actually had reason to suspect there had been some disruption in Julie life, so I attempted to engage in conversation. I was correct and found a willing partner.

Before continuing the story, let me share two principles that guide me:

- A reasonable assumption to make is that every person you ever meet deals with pain and suffering sooner or later.
- Our current cultural moment requires, more than ever, thinking relationally versus transactionally.

Fortunately for me, God's given me a heart to just love where they're at…and no one wants to be a project, anyway.

After a bit she asked how I was, and I mentioned that I'd be away at seminary for a bit. But the look on her face told me that the word "seminary" didn't mean much to her, so I elaborated a bit about loving Jesus. And that's when she exclaimed, *"You're a Christian? You don't look like a Christian!"*

No, I didn't ask what she thought a Christian should look like. But in a way I was glad she thought so, and here's why: because I wasn't dismissed out of hand.

You might remember from our recent trip through 1 Corinthians Paul writing to that messy church. In a way, they were struggling with what being Christian looks like, too. And Paul was helping them out, kinda in their business a little bit, described part of his motivation like this:

> Although I am free from all and not
>   anyone's slave, I have made myself a
>   slave to everyone, in order to win
>   more people. To the Jews I became
>   like a Jew, to win Jews; to those
>   under the law, like one under the law
>   —though I myself am not under the

law—to win those under the law. (1
Corinthians 9:19-20, CSB)

Obviously Paul isn't talking about clothing and hairstyles here,
but I think it's safe to say that he'd agree with this: if something
about how you show up is off-putting, "become like them" (in a
way that's appropriate). You wouldn't be an ambassador to
another country without attempting to learn their language
and culture, right? In a way that's true when you show up for
Jesus.

And this is even true where we go to work. Is the culture and
language in the medical industry the same as in the tech
industry? Nope. How about from one company to the next
even in the same industry? Nope.

In one odd little way, the same was true in my conversation
with Julie at the grocery store. It turns out she has zero
background in anything religious. She's not stupid, she just
hadn't lived in circles where the word seminary was in use. And
she'd never been to church, but for whatever reason, her sense
of what a Christian looks like obviously was different than
me…on the outside. But what she encountered was Jesus-who-
cared from the inside. In fact, it's *because* she wasn't on alert that
she let me in a little relationally.

So if there's maybe one little encouragement I'd like to leave
you with today, it's this. If for any period you've had any
exposure to churchianity, you've probably heard that we're all
called to be representatives or witnesses or ambassadors, right?
That's good stuff for your head.

But I'd like to also encourage you that, along with your head,
your heart and hands are also right where you are for a reason.

Being a missionary isn't just for those who go to Mexico or Mozambique. God love the people that do, but that's not most of us. Yet God's got a call on you and your life in just the same way. Most people aren't going to pastor a church or go overseas, but you've still got the privilege of being an ambassador of love...bringing something on the inside (the Holy Spirit) that will be seen on the outside as a you love, serve, and give.

Paul was uniquely adaptable – be like a Jew to the Jews, a Roman to the Romans. And maybe you are too, but that's not most of us. In fact, when you just show up and love on people, being intentional relationally about loving on them by serving them and being genuinely interested, you might just sometimes have someone notice that you don't look like a Christian...on the outside...only to have them see something different when you show up like one on the inside.

WHEN JESUS THE IMMOVABLE ROCK ON THE INSIDE, YOU CAN SHOW UP ADAPTABLE ON THE OUTSIDE.

14

BREATHING TOGETHER

PSALM 145:5-7

FOR TWELVE YEARS, SHE WORKED CLEANING OUT SEWERS. THE reason she had this job? She had was a Christian – the *only* Christian – in a village that was well-steeped in the communism of China. Yet when she met some Christians who visited – the first Christians she'd seen in years – and they offered her some new clothes, she said she didn't care about clothes. She wanted a Bible.

Hey hopeful, welcome to ForTheHope's Sunday Reflection where we pause from our read-through-the-Bible-in-a-year time to contemplate life in a little different way.

I had the good fortune a couple summers ago to spend Five weeks in Oxford England, focusing only on sharing Jesus. study evangelism and apologetics at the Oxford Centre for Christian Apologetics. Michael Ramsden, John Lennox, Os Guinness, Andy Banister, and a host of other great evangelists shared their stories, but in this one moment, it was my time with John Bechtel who struck me. And there's a lesson here for you, too.

John had grown up in China and been a missionary there his whole life. But this story of the lady wanting a Bible left me with a quivering lip and tear in my eye.

Remember, this lady hadn't just worked in the sewers for twelve years...she hadn't seen another Christian nor a Bible for twelve years. Bechtel, it turns out, went to this village and, in a deal with the mayor who wanted something, asked to meet the Christians in town. She was the only one.

The missionaries loved on her, worshiped with her, and encouraged her. And they left stunned at her love for the lord despite her unspeakable isolation and the fact that she just wanted a bible.

Well, there's one more interesting twist to the story, but I'll share that in a minute. Because I want you to ponder this: where would you be if you found yourself with no access, so to speak, to Jesus, except what you remember in your head?

And could it even be that in our information-overwhelmed western world, that we take that for granted. Could it be that sometimes the danger we face is the risk of familiarity? That we have so much access to having our souls fed in community and bible reading and various media sources that we risk losing our awe for God?

Maybe, then, the following warning is for us. The great Princeton theologian and preacher B.B. Warfield once gave a rather interesting warning to his theology students. He said:

 We are frequently told, indeed, that the great danger of the theological student lies precisely in his constant contact with divine things. They may come to seem common to him because they are customary.

Remember, this was at the turn of the 1900s! Continuing...

 … The words which tell you of God's terrible
majesty or of his glorious goodness may come to
be mere words to you—Hebrew and Greek words,
with etymologies, inflections and connections in
sentences. The reasonings which establish to you
the mysteries of his saving activities may come to
be to you mere logical paradigms, with premises
and conclusions, fitly framed, no doubt, and
triumphantly cogent, but with no further
significance to you than their formal logical
conclusiveness.

God's stately steppings in his redemptive processes
may become to you a mere series of facts of
history, curiously interplaying to the production of
social and religious conditions and pointing
mayhap to an issue which we may shrewdly
conjecture: but much like other facts occurring in
time and space which may come to your notice. It
is your great danger. But it is your great danger
only because it is your great privilege.

*...The very atmosphere of your life is these things; you
breathe them in at every pore: they surround you, encompass
you, press in upon you from every side. It is all in danger of
becoming common to you! God forgive you, you are in
danger of becoming weary of God!*[1] (emphasis mine)

So what should we do? I like the words of Brother Lawrence, a
17th century monk, who wrote a little work called the "Practice
of the presence of God." I like those how those words hang
together: "practice the presence of God."

Maybe as we reflect, it's a good time to remember that one of the primary means by which we practice the presence of God is to listen to the words of this God who speaks, this God who chose to reveal himself in the books of nature and scripture, this God whose plan not only included sending his sone on a rescue mission, but capturing those words in a book we read here every single day. And for that very reason.

> I will speak of your splendor and
> glorious majesty
> and your wondrous works. They will
> proclaim the power of your awe-
> inspiring acts, and I will declare your
> greatness. They will give a testimony
> of your great goodness and will
> joyfully sing of your righteousness.
> Psalm 145:5-7, CSB

So back to our lady in China. Amazingly, deprived of nearly every means of being connected to Jesus, by the power of the Holy Spirit she found meaning in her labor, beauty in serving in sewers. She found a way to practice the presence of God at work. And this meditation itself deepened her love for Jesus so much that, upon being given a choice of creature comforts, she asked for a Bible.

There's a fun twist in the story. It turns out that at that time the Chinese government let missionaries in, but they'd count the Bibles they brought into the country and make sure that's how many they left with. So what John and team did was to take an exacto knife to their Bibles, taking pages from a bunch of different bibles so as to reconstruct part of the New Testament to leave with this lady.

I don't know about you, but to me it's a reminder of the risk of familiarity that BB Warfield was warning about. It's the risk of taking for granted the sense of awe that is kindled in us when we really connect with God by pause reflect on his words to us.

We can go weeks without food, maybe days without water, but we can't go minutes without breath. And maybe, just maybe in a little reflection here in our time together, we can be encouraged to once again count him more precious than even our breath, renewing our strength to rise up like eagles on the awe of the very breath he's given us. And when God tells us that Scripture is God-breathed (2 Timothy 3:16), I love the idea that we do that breath-to-breath. In dialogue. Proclaiming His greatness, in a sense, by breathing together.

BRINGING GOD'S PRESENCE TO OTHERS MEANS BREATHING TOGETHER WITH HIM.

15

WORDS

LUKE 18:18-19

THERE'S AN OLD QUIP AMONG MARKETERS THAT IS RELEVANT not just to business:

 People don't by drills, they buy holes.

And this has a lot to do with the state of conversation in today's world, online and off. So for today's reflection, can I just encourage you with a couple ideas that might help us together, grow in the direction of Jesus?

Hey hopeful, welcome to #ForTheHope's Sunday Reflection where we pause from our read-through-the-Bible-in-a-year time to contemplate life — and even words — in light of God's story.

Let's start with a debate that is safe because it's foreign to most people at church. Living among us are those whose world is parsing words like philosophers and theologians, and in a time not long ago one of the trends in the world of ideas was debating the idea of atheism. Is atheism a lack of belief in

God, the absence of something? Or is it a positive affirmation, a truth claim that one should have to defend once stated?

Generally speaking, the one making a truth claim is the one on the hook for the burden of proof. "Prove there's no God" was argued from one side, and the other side said "Prove there IS." And they get bogged down in defining God and facts and the definition of proof versus reasonable inference from the evidence and... oh my.

Now hang with me, I trust this'll come home. Remember, people don't buy drills, they buy holes.

What is it that is really the argument above? What's really at stake if there is or isn't a God?

My point here isn't even to make that point, so much as to point out that sometimes words are a distraction relative to what you really want to get at.

A couple other examples:

What does "evangelical" mean? Actual research shows that most people – including Christians – don't know. Which is how it has gotten coopted to mean something political.

What about the words conservative or liberal? Same thing. They mean something different when talking about politics versus theology.

So what do we do about that? Well, what did Jesus do?

- Sometimes he answered questions, sometimes he refused to.
- Sometimes he spoke in parables, other times he didn't.
- Sometimes he answered a question with a question, sometimes he didn't.

So it's obvious there's no simple formula. Which makes a lot of sense…it's not typically useful to reduce people or communications to simple formulas anyway.

Remember, our idea here is "People don't buy drills, they buy holes." They think they want drills, and to a degree, they do. But what they want is an outcome. The point is one of getting to the heart or goal or desire behind the words.

Think about what Jesus did as recorded in Mark, Matthew, and Luke, what you might remember being called the rich young ruler

> A ruler asked him, "Good teacher, what
> must I do to inherit eternal life?"
> "Why do you call me good?" Jesus asked
> him. "No one is good except God
> alone." (Luke 18:18–19, CSB)

Now if you're looking for the main point of the passage, you'll remember that the wealthy young guy went away sad because his heart level issue was his love of his money. But I'm focusing on how Jesus challenged what he meant by the word "good."

The ruler's definition was keeping the rules. Jesus rattled off some of the ten commandments, and the guy's going "yup, been there, done all that!"

But along the way the young guy missed that if no one is good except God, then it'd have been weird to call Jesus good unless he was, in fact, God.

So if there are no formulas here, and we know that what people often don't really know what the words atheism or conservative or liberal or other things mean in a Scriptural sense, what do we do?

Get to the ideas and heart behind their question. They're talking about drills, but you want to discern holes.

Here's an example by way of a quiz of sorts. How would you answer the following questions?

- Like the rich young ruler asking " what must I do to inherit eternal life," do you believe that spiritual lives need to be transformed through an experience of trusting and following Jesus as Lord and Savior?
- And do you believe that that is because of the sacrifice of Jesus on the cross as making it possible the redemption of humanity?
- Do you think we should have high regard for, and even obey the Bible as God's word and authority?
- And when the Bible says Jesus followers, wherever they find themselves, should also take action to be missionaries and advocates for social good, do you agree?

If you answered "yes" to all four questions, you just fit the description of one of those words the world doesn't understand. Those four questions are the general characteristics of what historically it has mean to be *evangelical*.

Remember, the word evangelical comes from the greek meaning "good news." It's not good advice, like it's just a superior philosophy or methodology. How are lives ultimately saved and transformed? When they respond to the free gift offered by what Jesus did, and then being transformed from the inside out in a way that's not possible without the Holy Spirit. That's good news, indeed.

Is it true that people who affirm those four questions *tend* to vote one way versus another? Yes. Is it true that people who affirm those four questions *tend* toward one political party versus another? Yes.

Can you see how this gets messy?

That's one of many potential examples, and to keep today's reflection from being an hour, I'll stop there, except for reiterating this point: People buy drills, but they want holes. There's a motivation and heart behind what they say and do. It's an imperfect analogy, but it makes the point...the word evangelical could actually get in the way of you figuring out what someone really means.

Relative to the example I gave, some people in the church have stopped using the word evangelical for just this reason. Some argue that we shouldn't. And I'd argue that we need to pick and choose, because the point isn't the word. Whether the word is evangelical or atheist or critical race theory or any of a bunch of other words, the point is the ideas behind the word when you're not exactly speaking the same language.

The goal, after all, is clear communication to move people one notch closer to Jesus.

WHEN IN DOUBT, AVOID THE CHURCHY WORDS.

16

QUESTIONS OF WORSHIP

WITH WILLIAM TEMPLE

IF YOU LOOK UP THE WORD "WORSHIP" IN A TYPICAL SECULAR source, it's likely that it's defined, at least in relationship to the Christian worldview, a bit simplistically as

- show reverence and adoration for (a deity); honor with religious rites
- take part in a religious ceremony
- with the reverence and adoration appropriate to a deity.

But what if the Christian perspective is a whole lot more rich than that? I think it is.

As regards today, if we serve Jesus by serving others (and we do), might the Christian idea of worship touch down in how we talk with people?

Hey Hopeful, welcome to the Sunday reflection where we pause from our daily Bible reading to consider our life stories in the context of God's story. And today our journey will be to first share with you my favorite, rich definition of worship, briefly explore how each part informs our story, and then share a couple insights about what to ask or say when this touches down in day to day life.

In the first half of the last century, an Anglican priest named William Temple wrote this as his expression of what it means to worship Jesus:

> *Worship is the submission of all of our nature to God. It is the quickening of the conscience by his holiness; the nourishment of mind with his truth; the purifying of imagination by his beauty; the opening of the heart to his love; the surrender of will to his purpose--all this gathered up in adoration, the most selfless emotion of which our nature is capable.* ~William Temple

Whoah. That's powerful. And rather counter-cultural! Let's start with that first line.

Worship is the submission of all of our nature to God

I don't know about you, but when the first commandment is a command – don't have any other gods before me – and the Bible talks a lot about idolatry, it's easy to think externally. Am I making money or a relationship or something else my idol, the source of my hope?

But there's something more core to the matter. Idolatry comes from our own bent away from God, starting with who gets to rule my life. Who gets the final and ultimate say? Submission isn't exactly a popular word, particularly in a world that tells you the ultimate evil is inequality. So it's a big deal, a costly deal, to say that you'll give up being God in your finances, relationships, sexuality, or whatever else is the place you struggle with giving up control.

It is the quickening of the conscience by his holiness

Notice whose holiness it is. It's sure not mine! But I think it's important that this follows submission. God's not forcing you to love him. It wouldn't be love. So that submission we were just talking about is a prerequisite to him transforming your conscience – which means it's possible to dull your conscience, too. Want to know what God's will is? Enable him to quicken your conscience by his holiness.

Of course, holiness isn't exactly something talked about culturally, unless in a pejorative "holier than thou" sort of way. But holiness, *his* holiness, is complete set-apartness, purity, goodness, light. In Revelation 15:4 the angels sing, "You alone are holy," and yet elsewhere God commands us to be holy like he is? Learning to have our consciences quickened, learning to know God's will, learning to think God's thoughts after Him can only come through the power of the Holy Spirit received when we fully trust Jesus via belief and repentance.

the nourishment of mind with his truth

The Bible doesn't separate belief and action. You can't have true experience without true truth (as Francis Schaeffer used to say), and true truth is marked by action as even Jesus himself said. Nourishment? Think junk food. You are what you eat.

the purifying of imagination by his beauty

Remember how Paul writes to the Philippians about setting their minds on the good, true, and beautiful (Philippians 4)? That, of course, first is God. And how do we know Him? In the books of nature and scripture – the way he chose to reveal himself -- and then finally in His Son (Hebrews 1).

Since He's not only Creator, but also Sustainer of the cosmos, all that's good, true, and beautiful emanates from Him. For example, do bad people sometimes do good things? Yes, it doesn't mean they're good compared to a perfectly holy God, but it gives us something to focus on. Does art or music scream God's glory? It can (though I'd say it can be misused, too). But notice what Temple says here – worship includes having your imagination purified by God's beauty. Another good food vs. junk food moment.

the opening of the heart to his love

We do love to say, "God is love?" don't we? But do we stop to think about what love means? Does love mean accepting all ideas as equally true or all actions as ok? Does love mean that wrong doesn't have consequences? Of course not. So what does it mean that worship is the opening of the heart to His love? It means receiving, not achieving. It means discerning, not determining.

the surrender of will to his purpose

This is, in a way, subsumed in the opening statement about all of our nature, but let me refine that with a distinction. The Christian worldview says we are souls with bodies, both created good in the beginning, both now stained. But just like our bodies have appetites, some holy and some not so holy, so do our souls, and your will is part of your soul. So worshipping via surrendering your will is actually like what Jesus modeled: "not my will, but yours be done."

all this gathered up in adoration, the most selfless emotion of which our nature is capable

We get to Temple's final line, and what's the outcome? When you're in love, you learn to adore things that maybe you didn't even realize before – the way your lover greets a stranger, the sound of their voice, how their breathing changes when they falls asleep, whatever.

But our hearts are fickle (another biblical concept), so the Bible also talks about a different kind of love – not of what we feel but what we do, *agape*, self-*less* love. The kind of love that works at and on it, the kind that doesn't give up, the kind that puts the other first – sometimes when they *don't* deserve it (or particularly when they don't). But take your eyes off them, and put them back on Jesus. He always deserves it, he'll never let you down, he IS good and beautiful and true and trustworthy and faithful and all the things you want in a relationship. Get to know the real Jesus, and you can't help but adore Him.

So if serving Jesus is manifested in serving others, how might we talk with them? Notice I'm assuming here that we're following His command to, as we are going, being prepared to talk to them about him, for the hope that lies within us. So what might we say? I'm going to leave you with three simple questions, and I'll repeat them.

Why are you asking? I'm curious, why do you ask that?

Remember Jesus didn't always answer the question. So what's the motive behind the question? Sometimes it's genuine. Sometimes it's just a form of trickery or attack. Why are you asking? Why do you ask that?

What do you mean by that? Tell me more.

The oldest trick in the book from The Enemy is to change the meaning of something, including taking Scripture out of context. In broader culture, often that just bubbles up in someone you're talking to defining something differently than you do. Hot buttons are topics like tolerance or justice or evangelical or even or especially Jesus.

How'd you arrive at that idea?

Sometimes they're genuinely searching, and sometimes they're just repeating something someone else said (which isn't necessarily always bad). But it's useful to understand where they're coming from so you can meet them where you're at.

What does it mean to submit our nature and surrender our will in worship? To have our consciences quickened, imaginations transformed, and adoration fueled? How do we do that?

Worship isn't just a song we sing on Sunday morning. It's not only learning to fall more in love with Jesus, but learning to love the people in His world. Yes, we feed them and otherwise minister to physical needs, but that's exactly what puts us in a place to open up a conversation. What do you mean by that? How'd you arrive at that idea? Why are you asking?

Just asking these questions itself can be form of worship.

ASKING QUESTIONS WHEN YOU SHOW UP CAN ITSELF BE A FORM OF WORSHIP.

RAMON

MATTHEW 25:44

We weren't allowed to touch. We weren't allowed to take pictures. *"It's important,"* they said, *"to treat them like people, not projects."*

I get it. Homeless people *are* people. But I naturally touch people, even strangers, to communicate something to them. Pictures? They're not trophies to me. They're reminders, often as prompts to again feel again what was felt at the moment they were taken, something that's especially useful when you want to "get back there" emotionally.

The instructions came in the time leading up to my moment of deployment as a volunteer with a ministry to homeless people under the bridge in my hometown. I was happy to follow the rules, even if they felt counter to who I am.

After orientation we were asked to sign up to work at a particular station. I chose the book table. My hope was that this might be a place to talk to people about ideas. Other stations served food or gave haircuts or handed out clothing. All good. But I wanted to talk to someone.

As you might imagine, when someone would approach the table they'd look to see what was there. If I was going to talk to someone, I needed to draw them into a conversation and actually be genuine about it. Fortunately my life has prepared me for just that…to be able to greet complete strangers, and doing so with a heart full of love.

"How's that salad?" I'd say, pointing to a bowl of pasta salad one lady was carrying.

"Beautiful dog!" I exclaimed to another.

I wasn't alone working the book table. Sometimes the only thing I could do is sit back and stay out of the way.

Sometimes I would pray for the conversation that one of my peers was having. Sometimes I'd see someone a ways away and just pray for them.

"What kind of stuff do you like to read?" I asked one man.

He told me he liked reading about healthy living. I learned that he tried to do the right thing, even as he lived in a way that meant he didn't get to be very choosy about what he ate. He also said he liked to read stuff that tried to figure out how we got here, stuff like Stephen Hawking's ideas about where the universe came from. I paused. My instinct was to want to tell him about Jesus, but I hadn't earned the right.

I made more small talk. He was holding a ticket with a number on it, one I learned was his place in line to get some clothing. He said he didn't get to shower often, so he'd get clothing so he could wear something clean. He'd "donate" what we has wearing so it could be washed and recycled back to someone else who needed it.

It was the one conversation I had that night that had a real connection. At one point my arm raised, unconsciously, to put my hand on his shoulder. I stopped. Ooops! That was almost a rules violation.

If people are to be people and not projects, relationship is important. I didn't know if I ever would be back, but I decided that even a short interaction is a form of relationship.

I teach people about relationship in a professional context. Relationship starts in the heart. It also starts with a name.

Learning someone's name humanizes them. And like faces and voices, we get dialed into names at a very young age.

It's the opposite of the dehumanization that happens when we look at people in terms of faceless groups. In all of history, one way that oppressors wage wars is to lead their people to look at another group in a way that dehumanizes them. It's easy to look at Hitler and see what he did. It's less easy to look at ourselves and admit that we have our own version of "all homeless people are…" or "most black people are…"

There were lots of instructions that night, and the 'rules' were for the safety of the volunteers and those being served alike. All good, all positively motivated. Still, though, I was struck with this one thing that seemed most foundational, more essential than all of them: to ask for someone's name, their identity that's attached to all of who they are, their story. I knew this is what I wanted to do. It's what I *had* to do.

I didn't get to take a picture so I could remember how badly I want to serve people and perhaps be prompted to do so again. I didn't get to say "love you" by putting my hand on his shoulder. But then I remembered to do the one thing, the One Thing, that I could do and would remember.

"I'm Roger," I said. "What's your name?"

"Ramon, " came the reply.

I'd love to tell you that at that moment the heavens opened and we were greeted by a host of singing angels. But it was not to be.

Still, I couldn't help but think about Jesus' words when, on the day of judgment, there's someone standing before the Judge going,

> Lord, when did we see you hungry or
> needing clothes and not help you?
> (Matthew 25:44)

To some he'll say, *"Truly I tell you, whatever you did not do for one of the least of these, you didn't do for me."*

To others he'll say, *"Hey, you were pretty awful at the book table that one time, but I told you that you don't have to be awesome for me to work through you. Why don't you come over here? I want you to meet my friend Ramon."*

EVERY PERSON HAS A NAME. SHOW UP AND *ASK*.

18

BOYED CHEESE SANDWICHES

JOHN 3:16

"DAD, WHEN WE GET HOME I WANT A BOYED CHEESE SANDWICH!"

Yes, you read that correctly. boyed. Pronounced "boid." You'll see why in a moment.

"Huh?" I said to my young son who was sitting in the backseat of the car.

We were on our way from home. He was hungry. And he was letting me know his preferences, which he again affirmed.

"I want a boyed cheese sandwich."

I inquired further. Or rather, I probably grunted, "Boyed?"

It took a bit of additional prodding to figure out what he meant. He wanted grilled cheese sandwich…what thought he'd heard called a *girled* cheese. He just didn't want the feminine version. He wanted the boy version…a *boyed* cheese sandwich.

As humans, we can't help but hear what we hear in light of what we already know. It's particularly true for adults (who generally know more stuff than kids). It's part of why andragogy – the study of adult learning – is distinct from the more general idea of pedagogy, the method or practice of teaching.

So today is National Grilled Cheese Day…but it also happens to be Easter Sunday, the day when Christians celebrate the resurrection of Jesus of Nazareth.

And isn't it curious how our relationship to Easter (and Jesus) is also sometimes shaped by what we think we've heard or know?

As I've been in grad school studying a segment of theology that attends to evaluating and defending the truth claims of Christianity versus other truth claims, I've grown to not be surprised at how many Jesuses there are.

Some think he was a good moral teacher, some think he was a charlatan. Some accept him as a prophet but most certainly not God incarnate. Still others think he didn't even exist (despite the preponderance of even skeptical and atheistic scholarship which accedes to the evidence that he at least existed).

Let's start at the start: truth is that which accords with reality. If someone tells me it's raining outside, whether it is or isn't is not my opinion, however sincere I am at asserting what I think (I could be sincerely wrong).

So how's this Jesus thing connect to boyed cheese?

Religion is all about what humans do. It's about achievement… getting to god, or moksha, or nirvana, or financial success, or self-actualization, or…

Christianity is diametrically the opposite.

It's not about what we do. The good news is that our Creator knew we couldn't fix ourselves. We can't achieve our way to

God, so God sent Jesus on a rescue mission for us. Because for all our chasing, all our accolades, all our money, all our movements and causes, he knows we still are missing something. It's a "something" that religion and religiosity don't fix.

It's not that money or causes or trying to be a better person are wrong, of course, but these things of temporal value can't fill the place in our life that can only be filled when we're restored in relationship to the one who made us. Jesus, a loving Savior, longs to heal and restore your joy when you trust him. And in a world full of angst still striving fruitlessly to achieve, there is no more profound message of hope than looking to the very roots – the Creator of us all — to receive new life and eternal significance. In other words, it's new life *received*, not *achieved*.

And it all hinges on the resurrection, the very thing Christians remember and celebrate on Easter. It's true, and it's also beautiful.

To badly paraphrase one of Jesus' contemporaries, Paul, either the resurrection happened, and Jesus is, in fact God, or we Christians are idiots and fools (1 Corinthians 15:14).

And to badly paraphrase CS Lewis, this means Jesus was either loonie off his meds, the greatest con artist ever, or, in fact, Lord.

When we encounter Jesus, we encounter Truth and Beauty through the lens of what we knew before. Kinda like my son thinking what he heard was "girled" cheese. But what we think we know or the Jesus we'd make up doesn't change the truth that's "out there" (like the whether it's raining or not).

There are a lot of ideas about Jesus and religion floating around. But if there's a God who chose to create us and launch the rescue mission we celebrate on Easter, then it's not people's opinions that define who he is or what he's done.

As John, one of Jesus' followers and an eyewitness of the resurrection put it:

> For God loved the world in this way: He gave his one and only Son, so that everyone who believes in him will not perish but have eternal life. For God did not send his Son into the world to condemn the world, but to save the world through him. (John 3:16, CSB)

If true, it changes everything.

If not, I'm an idiot...and should be celebrating National Grilled Cheese Day instead of Easter.

Boyed and girled cheese sandwiches after (online) church, anyone?

WHAT DOES THE PERSON YOU'RE WITH "HEAR" WHEN THEY THINK ABOUT JESUS?

19

WHAT TO ASK AN ATHIEST

1 PETER 3:15

THERE IS A TIME TO BE A WITNESS. AND TO BE FAIR, THERE IS A time *not* to.

So how can you tell if you should do so?

It's useful to ask a question that determines their level of *openness*.

Let me share "the question," and then I'll share a story:

If God exists and Christianity was true, would you become a Christian? Why or why not?

I've asked this question of many people, but the story I'll share is related to a school project which required me to ask this of a stranger who identified as atheist. I'll share the dialogue as an example, and I ask "the question" at the end. At the end of this note I'll wrap with an important thing to remember.

Bill (not his real name) is a middle-aged man, a complete stranger to me, was introduced to me by a mutual acquaintance. In this case, I was on a mission for a school project, and for the project I was to begin by explaining that I was only going to ask questions – I'd not be responding or proselytizing.

He said, *"Good, because I'd just hang up on you – it would upset me."*

I asked why, and it was because he'd have felt misled – like I'd done a bait and switch.

What's your belief about God?

I learned Bill is an atheist and believed in no "being" or "consciousness." He believed God is an invention that helps explain life's difficulties, feel better about things like death, and have explanations for things mysterious like why we're here and what our purpose is.

How did you come to that conclusion?

Bill had no "experience," per se, to turn him off to religion. He cited education (college) as the reason for being atheist – being exposed to science and mythology specifically. He considers himself a person of rational thought.

Bill did have an experience in childhood of going to what sounded like it might have been vacation Bible school – his best friend growing up had highly religious parents who were also abusive. He said he did *not* correlate the two and even said so before I pressed more deeply. I listened reflectively to make sure I understood – he said those parents were religious and abusive, *not* abusive because they were religious. Reflecting on his childhood, he said he has never had faith.

Do you find your worldview meaningful and satisfying? Why or why not? In what ways?

"Satisfying? No," he said, *"the opposite. You die and that's that – what meaning is there in that? In fact, I'm jealous of those that do have that."*

I pressed in, and he explained that meaning is self-created. His self-created meaning: *"just to be of service, make the world better by my actions and example."*

Bill didn't mention a specific event, but I sensed that he had experienced something recently enough to be still feeling it. The reason: Bill mentioned that it *would* be comforting to have "God" to help deal with the "horrible feeling when you lose someone" if you could "comfort yourself that they're in a better place" and "you'd see them again."

What is your view on the Judeo-Christian God/Jesus/Christianity/the Bible/Christians? What do you think about the current direction of culture, including religion in the public square?

"Views?" Bill said, *"I don't have any."*

He went on to say that we all have biases and said again that people have "boxes to put stuff in to explain life's complexity." He tries to respect others as religion is "a really personal thing, and who am I to judge?"

He continued saying he doesn't have a negative view of religion, therefore, but explained that it can be used to oppress *"like those people who show up at funerals with signs that say 'God hates fags,' but that's a minority of them."*

Yes, he actually said that, which is ironic given that I've sadly seen similar behavior.

I pressed in. Bill free-associated that the Bible has been used to persecute women, conduct witch hunts, and deny LGBTQ people the ability to "be recognized as fully human beings with a right to be who they are."

Conversely, Bill acknowledged (almost wistfully) the value of community with others who have similar values and beliefs as it generates a "resiliency factor." Still, while he doesn't begrudge religious people their thinking, his belief that there is no God means he thinks prayer is "magical thinking" and that it's poppycock when some says they'll "send love and light."

Bill had already implied some of the "public square" perspective, so I asked if he thought it was more in the past or a current issue. He said that overall he thinks we're on a "trajectory in the right direction" as evidenced by some churches affirming LGBTQ leaders. He hopes the "'God hates fags' people go away and lose their power." Change, he thinks, causes some people to push back that and that such backlash is "from fear."

I closed the interview with "the question:"

If God exists and Christianity is true, would you become a Christian? Why or why not?

Bill paused. *"You mean like all that stuff in the Bible?"*

Then he continued:

"(Yes, but only) if God didn't hate gay people and women. But NOT if all that s*** in the Bible is true or there was a Satan. I guess it would depend on what kind of story it was; if God was benevolent and kind."

Bill paused. Then he laughingly said, *"I God was up to my standards, then I would."*

So what might we learn from this conversation with Bill?

First, by way of "the question," whose truth is Bill interested in? His own. Pursuant to "the question," *even if* God exists and Christianity were true, he's not interested.

Second, he saw the benefit of communities of faith. It's useful to remember that religious people *do* live longer[1] and are generally happier[2] (and this from secular research sources!). In another context, that might have been an interesting place to continue the dialogue.

Finally, Bill's response illustrates the usefulness of "the question." Bill's not interested in the Truth (capital T, if there is such a thing external to him). But he *does* long for what, ironically, God has wired him for (which, also ironically, is *because* of the one who is the way, truth, and life).

If I was in a place to be in relationship with Bill, that's exactly what I'd pursue…relationship. I would *not* attempt to correct Bill's misconceptions about God and the Bible until earning trust. If I did, I'm guessing he'd find a way to avoid me. The key, in my experience is that showing up must be genuinely relational, not transactional.

Instead, I think it's a good example of why the context of Peter's exhortation is so powerful:

> but in your hearts regard Christ the
> Lord as holy, ready at any time to
> give a defense to anyone who asks
> you for a reason for the hope that is
> in you. Yet do this with gentleness
> and reverence, keeping a clear
> conscience. (1 Pe 3:15-16a, CSB)

Do you remember who Peter is writing to? Christians who are suffering persecution. That word "defense" there is from the Greek meaning "to give an answer or response."

In other words, at some point people are going to wonder why you actually *do* have hope (confident expectation in the truth of the person and work of Jesus). And some who wonder will ask why.

Why don't you participate in office politics? Why do you go the extra mile for someone? Why do you shun the gossip going around? Why do you be nice to people who diss on you?

And how do they see that in you? Spending time together. When they know you are *relational* instead of *transactional*. When you actually, really care (which will begin to happen as your heart becomes more like Jesus' heart).

To be fair, there might be a time to walk away (which, ironically, this actually might be an act of love... go look up Romans 1:24).

But you'll never earn permission to share your reason for hope if you do. *Showing up is itself an act of love, even sacrificial love.*

Now...do we happen to know anyone who showed up and modeled sacrificial love for the sake of relationship?

Hmmm.... I wonder. Maybe we should remember that first and foremost. And then...

SHOW UP AND ASK, "IF CHRISTIANITY WERE TRUE, WOULD YOU BECOME A CHRISTIAN?"

20

PLUMS

JAMES 5:7-8

At the end of every summer — way back in the days of high school — my best friend and I would spend an afternoon reflecting — walking down to the nearby river and, along the way, stopping in an abandoned plum orchard. And those plums? Well, they were a little bit like life.

Hey Hopeful, welcome to #ForTheHope's Sunday Reflection where we pause from our Monday through Saturday reading-through-the-Bible-in-a-year time to consider life and work in a little different way.

We'll come back to plums and even a Bible verse here in a moment, but let me add a little twist.

Back in 2015 a friend and I began reading the Bible, out loud, to each other, every single day, *twice* a day. Sometimes it was for quite literally three or four stolen minutes while one of us was on vacation or standing in a line at an airport or in the hallway outside a concert, but in 957 days we only missed two of those appointments.

Along the way I got addicted to reading the Bible and started also doing it into this microphone. You see, like a lot of people, I *wanted* to be consistent with feeding on its living words every day, but it took community to do it. And now I have you, people who I know listen to the podcast.

Now you'd be a freak if you listened every single day like I (a freak) record every single day, but then as I always argue, we find time to feed our bellies…and when we *reeeeeally* start to find life in God's words, we start wanting to feed there more regularly, too. And here we are, now north of 1500 Bible reading episodes later, plus these Sunday reflections that I don't count in that number, plus other series like a couple for Advent. Probably pushing 1700 recordings.

Here's the point:

I don't say this for accolades…just as an encouragement. You see, we all are 1500 days older. And there's something about you that's stuck 1500 days ago because you didn't keep growing. But I'll bet there's also something for that's 1500 days better, too. And, Lord willing, something we'll both be 1500 days better at something 4.1 years from now. *So what do you want for yourself 1500 days from now?*

So back to those plums. Super late August or early September, they'd get getting ripe…or should I say, sort of. The trees would be full of them, and on the *outside* they all looked all plummy and yummy, but biting into one was the only way to know.

Now there were so many, if you bit into one that was still slightly sour from not being fully ripened, you'd move on until you found one that was sweet.

But that wasn't the end of our discovery. A plum could be sweet *and* not fully ripe. And how do you know? Well, if you ever find a *really* ripe plum, the middle of it's not holding on so tightly to the pit (the big seed in the middle). It's like it's ready to be eaten, ready to just fall away from that pit.

Now this may not be a perfect analogy, but the Lord's been teaching me patience in a new way this summer. And being a geek, I did a little study on the Bible's idea of patience and had myself a "doh!" moment. Yes, there are a lot of places in the Bible that speak to patience if not perseverance, but I hadn't stopped to think that the most patient character in the whole Bible is, oh, the star of the show, God himself.

For instance:

- Paul was getting in the bidness[1] of the church of Rome, asking rhetorically if they were going to get off their duffs with regard to sin: "Or do you presume on the riches of his kindness and forbearance and patience, not knowing that God's kindness is meant to lead you to repentance?" (Romans 2:4, ESV)
- Peter, writing to the scattered and persecuted church, says something similar, saying "The Lord is not slow to fulfill his promise as some count slowness, but is patient toward you, not wishing that any should perish, but that all should reach repentance." (2 Peter 3:9, ESV)

And there, my friends, is a key idea. Patience isn't just one of those things we should "learn to do." It's actually something that emanates from the very character of God – the God whose image we should be growing into.

Now here's the crazy thing. In the Bible the idea of patience is *less* frequently about how we *think* of it (a farmer waiting patiently for his crop to be ripe), and more frequently associated with hardship or suffering or persistence in the face of pain.

Yet often my life seems default to patience being about 'those dang crops not growing fast enough. In other words, the risk is that we are with someone who's not sweet (yet) and, like an unripe plum, toss them to the side.

It's easy to want to live life without pain, around pain, avoiding pain, instead of *through* pain. Not ripe moment? Not ripe person? Toss. Avoid. Move to another.

And here's the twist. In an orchard of infinite plums, you can do that – keep looking for the one that's perfectly ripe. But what does Jesus do? People aren't plums. He looks you in the eye, and says "I'll meet you where you're at, but I'm not content to leave you where you're at."

So what would it look like if we did the same thing?

We'd look at one person and see they're more ripe, but another person we'd realize is still sour, and another seems sweet on the outside but won't let you get to the middle – and if we were doing what Jesus does, we'd think a little more about meeting them where they're at and nurturing the process of ripening. We'd be more relational, less transactional.

My friends, I'm as guilty as the next person of not doing this so well. I am no hero. But if there's maybe one bit of encouragement for your today it's the way James put it:

> Therefore, brothers and sisters, be
>   patient until the Lord's coming. See
>   how the farmer waits for the
>   precious fruit of the earth and is
>   patient with it until it receives the
>   early and the late rains. You also

must be patient. Strengthen your
hearts, because the Lord's coming is
near. (James 5:7-8, CSB)

For me (and imperfectly I might add) that's being in the Bible
every single day so I have "extra spiritual food" I can share. It's
hard enough to walk in the peace of the Holy Spirit *with* that,
and it's nearly impossible without it.

Part of showing up, when it's relational, is "staying showed
up," looking for that next friend who wants to be on a journey
together, ripening together instead of kicking the sour ones to
the curb.

The Lord might have something different for you on your
journey, but may we all, like Jesus, get a little better at
nurturing plums.

SHOW UP AND "STAY SHOWED UP."

BOOKS

ACTS 1:8

IN BIBLE TIMES, THERE WAS NO PAPER AS WE THINK OF IT TODAY. And by one estimate I read, the cost of the whole Bible on scrolls and parchment in Jesus' day would have been the equivalent of $30,000 USD!

Fast forward nearly two millennia to the early 1900s, and there were still traveling libraries to brings books to regular people. Why? Because books (and access to knowledge) were still expensive in a relative sense. It's part of why steel baron Andrew Carnegie decided his part of his legacy libraries — he funded the founding of 3000 libraries before he died in 1919.

And what does this have to do with Jesus and the gospel and you and me?

Hey Hopeful, welcome to #ForTheHope's Sunday Reflection where we pause from our Monday through Saturday reading-through-the-Bible-in-a-year time to consider life and work in a little different way.

Access to books used to be the domain of the wealthy. Over time, as technology tends to affect things, they became less expensive. And historians often agree that the two most revolutionary inventions were, respectively, the moveable type printing press and the internet.

But what if books *again* become the domain of the wealthy in a different way? And might that give us as Christians a different way of seeing the world?

Sit tight, I'm going to get a bit academic on you for a moment, but I trust the winding road serves a purpose.

Communication at all presupposes the condition of mind and mode...a mind capable of encoding or sending a message, a mind capable of decoding or receiving a message, and common mode of communication – like language -- that's shared.

Indeed, one of the arguments for God's existence is that the "fine tuning" of universe (things like the complexity of DNA) make the chance of random combinations producing life and intelligence a mathematical joke.

In fact, a whole lot of things bear the marks of... language.Pastors and theologians even use a shorthand to even joke about it...the "books of Scripture and nature."

And you'll recall the Paul, in Romans, notes that people are without excuse because they knew God and chose to turn the other way. Why? Because whether in a sunset or in Scripture or in DNA, God's fingerprints are all over everything in a way that you have to purposefully ignore or try to explain away to get around. Even the best arguments that attempt it when limiting themselves to the known universe fall short, so they either say stupid things like "The universe must have created itself" (you don't need a PhD in astrophysics to see through that), or they say scary things like, "because everything is just time plus matter plus chance, life is meaningless" (which would be true if somehow the universe did manage to come into being without supernatural invention).

But you don't need an advanced degree to know, deep inside, that we aren't here for no purpose.

So back to books. If there's a God who could create something out of nothing, we'll call it the cosmos, then it stands to reason that miracles and raising someone from the dead and a virgin birth would be easy fare. *And so would partnering with humans to communicate through humans in a language that you and I could understand.* It's why we view the Bible as "inspired" and "the word of God." God can't err, so his words in the Bible (in its original copies) can't err.[1]

My point today isn't even about the Bible, though, it's to point out a distinction between the inspired word of God and other books that gives other books a proper place in your ministry of showing up. It's about the cultural condition we find ourselves in and what it means to love your neighbor. Sit tight.

Now I'm going to tell you about something I do, but please please please don't make me the hero of the story. Promise? I want *you* to see yourself in the story.

I have two boxes of books on various Christian topics in the trunk of my car – just so I can give them away. Part of your funding this ministry is used in that way. Even this book itself is going to be given away as much as possible (see those "anonymous" folks on the dedication page? If you're reading this for free, one of them made it possible).

So this book-giving aspect of my ministry of showing up has some examples that'll give you some context, but it's important to understand FTH's ministry philosophy first.

Human beings relate to the written word in a way that is psychologically and biologically unique. And this is also borne out in research between how people read actual books vs consuming content on the internet.

Furthermore, in a *relative* sense, the price of physical books is going back up. No, not in absolute terms, but in the sense that for many people, the perceived value of something tangible like a book is a LOT more than something intangible, like the internet. Give someone a website address, and unless they're seriously motivated to read it right then, poof! The point: *if you give someone a book, it's more likely they'll hang keep it.*

What's this mean for your ministry of showing up? Your potential impact is extended beyond the actual time you're together. Even if someone doesn't engage the book right then, it'll stay "in their space."

Those examples:

I was having coffee with a non-believer business acquaintance and the conversation turned to spiritual things.

"Would you be open to perusing a book?" I asked. "I won't grill you about it in the future, and whether you read it or not doesn't affect our friendship, but it'd answer some questions for you."

She said yes.

The win: Giving her a quality book that I know will answer her question(s) in a way that faithfully points her to the good news of Jesus. Notice, though, that the approach let her choose. Sometimes people say no.

A couple weeks ago at church I said hello to some new guys, and as it turns out, they were at church from a local recovery center. And it turns out that one of them is a brand new

Christian and really interested in the area of study where I got my master's degree…and just happen to have books in the trunk. So after church, his buddies and the center's chaperone waited while he and I went to the trunk of my car and I gave him two books. The win? Helping him engage quality material in a world where there is a lot of tripe.

A couple days ago I got a call from a podcast listener who'd moved recently to another state. Her family has had trouble finding a good church, and she distraught at what was being taught in a class at the church she thought – up to that point – was alright. True enough, it was seriously askew. I hopped on Amazon and sent her a couple books. The win? Helping him engage quality material in a world where there is a lot of tripe.

Now here's the thing. Could I tell them to read the Bible? Yes, I could have. Obviously I think rather highly of the Bible. *But they weren't all at that place in the journey, or their journey included questions that the Bible doesn't directly answer.*

That's worth saying again. The Bible has the answers for the *ultimate* questions in life — who is God, why are we here, who am I and what's my purpose, why is there evil in the world, where does all this go? But even Bible authors referred to other, non-biblical writings or cultural artifacts from time to time.

My friends, the goal is to be a catalyst for helping someone encounter God. And a book in their hands is a bit like getting a chance to keep showing up, and you know they have something from a Christian perspective.

Oh, and it doesn't have to be expensive. Start with one. That you found at a thrift store.

Books other than the Bible may not be the word of God, but that doesn't mean they don't communicate God's heart. Much like, I hope and pray, this book and podcast (if there's truth, it's God's, and any failure is mine).

In Acts 1:8 Jesus says

> But you will receive power when the
> Holy Spirit has come on you, and
> you will be my witnesses in
> Jerusalem, in all Judea and Samaria,
> and to the ends of the earth." (Acts
> 1:8, CSB)

Jesus is clearly not expecting that to happen just by the immediate group he's standing in front of. Some of them went on to write stuff down -- meaning their witness was not just spoken — and we ended up with the New Testament. Importantly, though, "to the ends of the earth" meant they were going to connect with people who connect with people who connect with people.

And that leads to you and me.

You, my friend, already have a ministry of reconciliation because you are a temple of the Holy Spirit (2 Corinthians 5:11-21). But you also know that mind didn't evolve from matter, rather, mind created matter, including you and me and language and books and opportunities. You, have been called to such a time as this.

KEEP A BOOK — OR EVEN A BOX OF THEM -- TO GIVE YOU A CHANCE TO "SHOW UP" BEYOND SHOWING UP.

22

SOUL EYES

1 SAMUEL 16:7

"ARE YOU...RICH?"

I was 9 years old. We'd just moved to Augusta, Georgia. The neighborhood was remote enough so that we lived on a dirt road. And one of the neighborhood kids approached me and started talking.

"Are you...rich?"

Hey hopeful, welcome to #ForTheHope's Sunday Reflection where we pause from our Mon-Sat reading-through-the-Bible-in-a-year time to consider life and work in a little different way.

To say I was surprised would have been an understatement. Rich? Us? My dad was in the Army, and my mom was a stay at home mom. Rich wasn't a descriptor I identified with.

I don't remember if I asked the kid why he asked that or not, but I remember his answer.

"Well, you've got a van and motorcycles."

True enough, my folks drove a van. And my dad and I each had dirt bikes. But apparently relative to my new neighbor's perspective, that was the domain of the wealthy.

As confusing as that was to me, it was his next question that most took me aback....

"Do you smoke?"

Now this was the 1970s, and my dad was in the military. I knew what smoking was all about. At least, I thought I did, and in my world nine year olds most definitely did not smoke.

When remembering that encounter, what strikes me is how I even think about it as I'm remembering it. If I'm honest, my first thought now is "What's a third grader doing smoking cigarettes?" And my second thought, putting on a little pastoral decorum, recalls God's words to Samuel.

 Humans do not see what the LORD sees, for humans see what is visible, but the LORD sees the heart. (1 Samuel 16:7b, CSB)

Remember, this is Samuel, one of the studliest prophets. He's on an errand to find the king that will replace Saul, and God leads him to Jesse and his crew. One by one, Jesse trots out his sons, and one by one God's like, "Nope, not that one." Finally Jesse runs out of sons...except for one not there because he was out tending sheep. David.

A lesson, even if not the main point of the passage, is that we as humans are fallible. Even Old Testament prophets. I mean, this is *Samuel*, but he still, kinda like a pastor at your church, happens to still see through human eyes sometimes or even most of the time.

Put another way, we *know* that God looks at the heart, but *we* often see *with* our eyes rather than *through* our eyes (and with our souls).

Recently I had an interview for a pastoral role at a church in the little town I live in outside Portland. And rather ironically, while I spent a lot of my years *sleeping* in this little outlying town and thinking of my life as in the city, even before this role came up I realize God has been working on my heart about this little community.

There is a darkness here. For instance, they go over the top with celebration for Halloween. Like, over the top. But perhaps even more telling, this summer I was doing regular walks on a loop around our rural fairgrounds, and more than once saw a hypodermic needle on the side of the road.

Now I don't have to tell you, people who use hypodermic needles for legit purposes aren't typically using them in cars and leaving them along the side of a country road.

And I have to ask myself...do I see a fifth grader who smokes, or a soul in pain? A hypodermic needle "loser" who's putting others in the community at risk, or a soul in pain? Am I looking *with* my eyes? Or *through* my eyes and with my soul?

You've probably heard the song by Brandon Heath on this very thing, and I love how the chorus turns it into prayer:

> Give me Your eyes for just one second
> Give me Your eyes so I can see
> Everything that I keep missin'
> Give Your love for humanity
> Give me Your arms for the broken-hearted
> The ones that are far beyond my reach
> Give me Your heart for the ones forgotten

Give me Your eyes so I can see

In the Samuel story, ol' Sam be like, "Whoah, surely this is the one!" But get this…interestingly enough, this wasn't an issue of sin on Samuel's part. I think it just reflects the fact that, even as we mature into abiding, maturing into staying tuned into the Holy Spirit's guiding, we're not going to get it right all the time.

The next verse in that Brandon Heath song reflects on doing the same:

> Step out on the busy street
> See a girl and our eyes meet
> Does her best to smile at me
> To hide what's underneath
> There's a man just to her right
> Black suit and a bright red tie
> Too ashamed to tell his wife
> He's out of work, he's buyin' time
> All those people goin' somewhere
> why have I never cared?

Let me leave you with that last line as encouragement, not condemnation: if you ever wonder why you sometimes do see with the eyes instead of the soul, that's evidence of the Spirit's loving conviction.

Becoming a Christian doesn't mean we instantly see like Jesus sees. And this side of glory, we *are* sometimes going to see grade school kids smoking cigarettes or roadside hypodermic needles litterers and be tempted to think "what's wrong with the world" instead of "I know what's wrong with the world, and it's me and it's sin and it's brokenness trying to fill a god-shaped hole in their hearts, and every one of us needs Jesus. And I *am* rich…but it's not because I own a motorcycle or even have a roof over my head…it's because the creator and sustainer of the universe is the king who cares."

Lord, give us your eyes for just one second, give us your eyes so we can see *through* our eyes and with our souls. We'll never be perfect at it, but we can't stop trying to see what Jesus sees.

MAKE EVERY EFFORT TO SHOW UP WITH SOUL EYES.

23

SURELY

1 CO 2:10-15

> Jack was my best friend and my big buddy my protector. My mentor. I really admired him. It was May 12th, 1944…

THE VOICE WAS EARNEST AND HONEST, JUST SHARING A MEMORY. The way you might share if you were just capturing memories into an old cassette tape recorder. Because that's what he was doing…Johnny Cash.

Hey Hopeful, welcome to #ForTheHope's Sunday Reflection where we pause from our daily Bible reading to consider our stories in light of God's story in a little different way. Today I want to talk with you about being sure. Particularly in light of this story I gleaned from a YouTube TV documentary I watched about Johnny Cash.

Here's Johnny talking:

> It was May 12, 1944, a Saturday morning. Jack and I would always go fishing together. I said, *"Go fishin' with me."*

And he said, *"No, I got to work. We need the money."*

He had a job cutting the Oak trees. I just remember my mother telling him something like, *"You don't feel like you should go?"*

and he said, *"I don't. I feel like something is going to happen."*

And she said, *"Please don't go."*

And I said, *"Go fishing with me. Let's go fishing."*

And he kept saying, *"I've got to go to work."*

And I went on down toward the fishin hole and here comes my father in a car with the preacher. I knew something was really bad wrong. Dad took a bloody brown sack. He pulled Jack's clothes out of that bag and showed me where the table saw got him, cut him from his ribs down all through his stomach. And that was the first time I ever saw my dad cry. And he said, *"Come on into his room and say goodbye to him."*

My mother was right at the head of his bed. Jack kept calm, and looked around and he said, *"I'm glad you're all here."* And he closed his eyes and said, *"It's a beautiful river. It's goin' two ways."* He says, *"Oh mama, can't you see it?"*

She said, *"No son I can't see it."*

And he said, *"Or can you hear the angels?"*

And she said, *"No, I can't hear the angels."*

> Tears came out of his eyes, as he said, *"I wish you could. They're so beautiful. And what a beautiful place that I'm going."*[1]

I never met Johnny Cash, but I can relate to his story about being sure of something that's true in one very real way, something I'm sure about. Here's why:

I had a dream or vision when I was five years old living in Seattle Washington, and somehow I believed it to be true. I even told my mom so.

Months later the scene I'd seen in my dream or vision unfolded in real life...6000 miles away in Okinawa, a tiny Japanese island just off the coast of China.

I can't explain it. But I can know that it surely happened to me. And as you might imagine, Johnny Cash wasn't trying to explain what happened. But he believed it to be surely true.

Today I want to reflect with you just a bit on what we know to be true, beginning with a passage in the Bible. And while today's not about a full biblical theology or exposition of the text, I trust you'll appreciate where we're going.

In Paul's first letter to the church in Corinth, he writes to them:

> Now God has revealed these things to us
>   by the Spirit, since the Spirit
>   searches everything, even the depths
>   of God. For who knows a person's
>   thoughts except his spirit within
>   him? In the same way, no one knows
>   the thoughts of God except the
>   Spirit of God.

> Now we have not received the spirit of the
>   world, but the Spirit who comes from
>   God, so that we may understand what
>   has been freely given to us by God. We
>   also speak these things, not in words
>   taught by human wisdom, but in those
>   taught by the Spirit, explaining
>   spiritual things to spiritual people.
> But the person without the Spirit does
>   not receive what comes from God's
>   Spirit, because it is foolishness to
>   him; he is not able to understand it
>   since it is evaluated spiritually.
> The spiritual person, however, can
>   evaluate everything, and yet he
>   himself cannot be evaluated by
>   anyone. (1 Corinthians 2:10-15 CSB,
>   formatting mine)

I once had a brief discussion with someone online. She was claiming that a particular psychological instrument was a good thing, and I pointed out that the originator of said psychological instrument said that he'd *received* it via automatic writing.

For those of you who know of new age and occultic practices, you'll know that automatic writing is contact with the spirit world — channeling, if you will. If you read the Bible, you'll know that 1 Jn 4:1 instructs us to test the spirits.

I pointed out that what she was pointing to as true was contrary to what the Bible said. Her response to me, *"But God told me it was true!"*

I didn't continue the discussion.

She was sure of herself, sure it was true. But here's the thing: If what she said was true, then the Bible was wrong. If the Bible was right, then she had to be wrong.

To be sure, there are some things in the Bible about which we are more sure, and some things which aren't as clear. But I want to leave you with this thought today:

If I said one thing, but I did another, you'd have a little head-scratching going on, right? And to be sure, there isn't a one of us that is perfectly consistent.

But what about God? Is what God said in his books of nature and Scripture perfectly consistent? Consistent with him, his nature, and how he speaks to us? (That's a rhetorical question, by the way. See below).

I like the way AW Tozer put it in his book, *Knowledge of the Holy*:

> I think it might be demonstrated that almost every heresy that has afflicted the church through the years has arisen from believing things that are not true, or from overemphasizing certain true things so as to obscure other things equally true. To magnify any attribute to the exclusion of another is to head straight for one of the dismal swamps of theology: and yet we are all constantly tempted do just that.
>
> For instance, the Bible teaches that God is love, and some have interpreted this is in such a way as virtually to deny that He is just, which the Bible also teaches. Others press the Biblical doctrine of God's goodness so far that it is made to contradict His holiness. Or they make His compassion cancel out His truth. Still others understand the

sovereignty of God in a way that destroys (or at least greatly diminishes) His goodness and love.

We can hold a correct view of truth only by daring to believe everything God as said about Himself." ~AW Tozer, Knowledge of the Holy

So back to me and my buddy Johnny Cash.

Was there anything about Johnny Cash's experience that was contradictory to God's revelation? No, I don't think there was.

How about mine? No. I can't explain it. To be sure my own experience doesn't reveal anything about God, per se, but it doesn't contradict the Bible, either.

Christian apologists – those who have a service ministry of defending the truth claims of Christianity – rest their ministry on the fact that God is, and philosophically, *has* to be perfectly consistent and truthful, or he wouldn't be perfect.

This includes, actually, defending why you can trust your contemporary English Bible. It doesn't mean we perfectly understand it, but it does mean that we can rest surely on the fact that it won't contradict itself when properly understood. And we have to trust that "true truth," as the great thinker Francis Schaeffer calls it, won't be in contradiction with it either (no matter what the source).

Believe me, I can understand wanting to know stuff surely. But I'll remind you – and myself, too – that there is *no* knowledge you have of anything outside yourself that you have 100% knowledge of. Importantly, we can know things *surely* even if we don't know them completely.

Sometimes, though, we worship the idol of understanding. And when something doesn't make sense, we trust ourselves more than we trust our Bibles…the Bible that is God's word, the words of God, the God who cannot and does not lie.

Sometimes we worship the idol of experience. Like the gal I chatted with on Facebook. "I KNOW it's true!"

To be sure, in one sense, I'm sure she believes that. Just like I know what I experienced when I was five years old.

But remember how, as we journeyed through Exodus recently (on the podcast, obviously), Pharoah's court magicians mimicked some of the miracles that God performed through Moses?

Remember how a couple of the main ways the Bible depicts the devil is as a deceiver, disguised as an angel of light?

As Paul wrote to the Corinthians, you can know something by the power of the Holy Spirit. Recall what we just read above:

> Now God has revealed these things to us
> by the Spirit, since the Spirit
> searches everything, even the depths
> of God. For who knows a person's
> thoughts except his spirit within
> him? In the same way, no one knows
> the thoughts of God except the
> Spirit of God. (1 Corinthians
> 2:10-11 CSB)

Did you catch that? Beyond your physical and mental means of knowing is your spiritual means of knowing. And Paul's argument is that the same Holy Spirit in you knows God's thoughts because, well, He is God.

But he continues.

> Now we have not received the spirit of
> the world, but the Spirit who comes
> from God, so that we may
> understand what has been freely
> given to us by God. (1 Corinthians
> 2:12 CSB)

Has he given us everything? No. Can we be sure about what
He has given us? Yes, surely we can. Continuing…

> … not in words taught by human
> wisdom, but in those taught by the
> Spirit, explaining spiritual things to
> spiritual people. [14] But the person
> without the Spirit does not receive
> what comes from God's Spirit,
> because it is foolishness to him; he is
> not able to understand it since it is
> evaluated spiritually. (1 Corinthians
> 2:13-14 CSB)

Again, my question back to you is, "Will God ever contradict
himself?" And if something doesn't make sense, who are you
going to trust?

Interestingly, one of the things that near death experiences like
the one Johnny Cash witnessed is a well-researched,
scientifically documented phenomenon. Which is an
interesting refutation of a naturalist or materialist world view
that believes that the material universe is all there is. At the
same time, the prophet Jeremiah (in what we refer to as
Jeremiah 17:9-10a)

> The heart is more deceitful than

anything else, and incurable—who
can understand it? I, the LORD,
examine the mind, I test the heart to
give to each according to his way,
according to what his actions
deserve. (Jeremiah 17:9-10a, CSB)

Here's what you can know for sure: God can't contradict himself, not just because the Bible says so, but because a perfect being would be non-contradictory. That would make no sense, like a square circle or a married bachelor. It'd be nonsense. We don't worship a God of nonsense.

You can know for sure that we can know some things surely, even if we can't know them fully. You don't need the Bible for that.

And we know for sure our own hearts are deceitful. We don't need the Bible for that.

And we know for sure therefore, that if God is good and true and beautiful and my experience contradicts the Bible, then I have a decision to make. Is my own experience the truth, or is the Bible?

We can idolize knowledge, and we can idolize experience. And what we're really doing is idolizing the trusting of ourselves over trusting God's revelation of himself in his word. Or it's the trusting of someone else's doubt — doubt that the God who created the universe could make sure that we have what we need to know he exists, know right from wrong, know we need a savior to reconcile that relationship (because we can't do it on our own).

There are plenty of things I'm unsure of, but of this I am sure that you can be sure:

If you have put your trust in Jesus, and if you ask him to reveal himself with an honestly seeking heart, he will. Just as sure as the fact that it may not be the way you expect it or when you want it. Just as I'm sure that as we read the Bible here on this podcast we won't understand everything.

But surely we can be sure of the important things. Just like Johnny Cash.

WHAT MIGHT HAPPEN IF WE ACTUALLY, REALLY TRUSTED WHAT WE CAN BE SURE OF?

GHOSTS

PSALM 34:8

IMAGINE THAT YOU ARE INVINCIBLE. WHAT WOULD YOU DO with your superpower?

I thought I was sorta invincible once. Of course, when you actually see a ghost like I did, well, that's the rest of the story.

Hey Hopeful, welcome to #ForTheHope's Sunday Reflection where we pause from our daily Bible reading to consider our life and work stories in light of God's story.

To be fair I didn't actually see a ghost. But the story is worth the telling.

One of my younger sisters and I were in a fort that we'd built, one that we were particularly proud of because it had — wait for it —multiple rooms. And for whatever reason one summer evening my mom let us keep playing out there until after dark. I was seven, and my sister was five, so being out after dark was a big deal, a real treat.

As the sun went down, though, it first got dark inside the fort. Thick-black-tar dark. And my sister got scared.

"See this?" I said, holding up a sizable stick. "I'll protect you."

I meant it, too. It was an awesome stick, and while I'm not sure invincible is the word I'd use to describe what I felt, I certainly had a double dose of confidence.

Unbeknownst to me, when it came time for us to be called in for the night, mom asked dad if he'd do the honors. He thought it would be funny to grab a bedsheet, throw it over his head, and, you guessed it, come around the corner doing his spookiest, *"Ooo, ooooooo!"*

Well, my sis shrieked. And 113% of any bravery I had just a few minutes prior drained out of me. We both bolted for the house.

I think this is a bit like what happens to us when we think about following Jesus. Jesus said, "follow me," and this was both an invitation and a charge. In one sense following him helps answer the deepest question in life about identity – we go from being followers of our own dead-end desires to being ambassadors for the King. And in another sense it opens up a new question: what does following Jesus look like?

One of those ways that we mention often on this podcast is His charge to all believers called the Great Commission. We are *ambassadors*. We are *called* to a task…as you are going, whether you're a mom or an employee or an entrepreneur…we're both his hands and feet in service to others, and we're his lips in saying, "Come and see." Jesus calls you to show up with head, heart, and hands.

Sometime it's easy to be really in love with Jesus and feel invincible and ready to do that serving and sharing. He is, after all, the epitome of sacrificial love. If he laid down his life for us, the least we can do is be his ambassador.

But it's also easy to, in a sense, to see a ghost and suddenly find yourself a little short in the moxie department.

I remember hearing the well-known apologist and evangelist Josh McDowell tell some of his story — a story that included everything from being abused as a child to dealing with his own spiritual doubt to getting thrown in prison – more than once – in some country not taking to kindly to a Christian showing up for Jesus. And he said a couple things that I think are useful for you, today, one of which was

 I never met anyone Jesus didn't die for. God loves the worst; can I do any less? ~ Josh McDowell

You may not be called to be an evangelist from a stage. Most Jesus-followers aren't. But we are supposed to love our neighbors. And loving those around you — those who have abandoned you, or your fellow employees, or that family member who talks behind your back, or those who don't like you because you don't vote like they do — with the love of Jesus as the ambassador He has asked you to be might be just quietly praying for them. And that's good.

Maybe it's going out of your way to serve them, perhaps even in a way that makes them scratch their heads. And that's good.

But if you're like most people, you've probably also had times when something prompted you to speak up…and you didn't. And I understand. It's natural, even, to want to be liked, understood, and even loved. I understand what it's like to be misunderstood, rejected without someone really getting to know you. Or even fear losing your job.

Just this last year I was having a conversation with my biggest client, and the conversation turned personal. At one point he went, "Wait, you aren't an *evangelical* are you?" It was almost a sneer.

The truth is, he has no idea what evangelical means…and his perspective is entirely shaped by the mess we commonly see around us (which should not surprise us, given that research shows that even most Christians don't even know the definition of evangelical).[1]

And the truth is I had a "life flash before your eyes" moment. I knew there could be a real cost when I said, "Yes."

Here's the thing about that cost of following Jesus and facing the occasional ghost, and I'll use the words of 20th-century pastor and theologian AW Tozer:

 What comes into our minds when we think about God is the most important thing about us. ~ AW Tozer

So what do you *really* think?

Jesus said, "I'll send God the Holy Spirit to comfort and counsel you and guide your words" (Acts 1:7-8, sorta). But we think, "I'm no evangelist."

Jesus said, "I'm the way and the truth and the life, and whether people realize it or not, their greatest suffering and need is to be reconciled with God" (John 14:6, sorta). But we think, "If I give them a meal, it's ok if I don't ever get all Jesus-y on them.

Jesus said, "You're a citizen of The Kingdom first, and that means you'll a stranger here" (Matthew 6:33, sorta).

But we think, "I've got something here to hang on to. And I've got a mortgage to pay. And what if my family think I'm nuts?"

Sometimes we don't bolt for the door exactly, but get into a dialogue with someone and offer what Dietrich Bonhoffer called "cheap grace." We don't tell others that Jesus actually said there'd be a cost to following him. We let them continue to think that fighting for racial justice or ending poverty or walking an old lady across the street *is* the gospel as opposed being something that flows *from* a gospel-shaped life.

The truth is I've done and said all those things. I'm not busting *your* chops. Been there, failed that myself.

As I listened to Josh McDowell tell his story, a couple other things he said struck me and still ring in my ears today.

His wife told him:

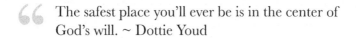 The safest place you'll ever be is in the center of God's will. ~ Dottie Youd

He went on to bring it home:

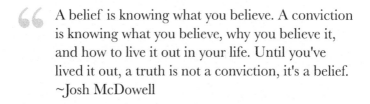 A belief is knowing what you believe. A conviction is knowing what you believe, why you believe it, and how to live it out in your life. Until you've lived it out, a truth is not a conviction, it's a belief. ~Josh McDowell

Read that last line again.

My friends, here's what God wants for you:

> Taste, and see that the Lord is good.
> Blessed is the person who takes
> refuge in him. (Psalm 34:8, CSB)

What comes to mind when you think about God? Is he safe and good and a source of strength and courage? He can be. He wants to be. He invites you to taste and see.

If I can be humbly presumptuous, God says to you,

"I know you're not invincible, and I know ghosts will come around the corner when you least expect them, and I know that you could actually lose your job or have your family think you're nuts for actually believing the Bible.

But I am enough. I am the strong tower. It's my world, and I'm the king, and all this like grass will pass away. But my word will never pass away, and an eternity with me in a sinless new heaven and earth will make all this world's temporary worries pale in comparison.

Now as you are going, as you're showing up, serve and share. There are others who I've ordained to hear my son's words — "follow me" — and you're part of how that happens. I've got your back in the way (that is the only way) that really, actually counts for eternity.

My child, show up today in light of eternity, because the Holy Spirit in you is greater than all those ghosts (1 John 4:4, sorta)."

WHAT IF YOU TRUSTED THE CREATOR AND KING ENOUGH TO SHOW UP?

NOTES

2. HOLY WORK

1. John Piper, *Sanctification in the Everyday: Three Sermons by John Piper* (Minneapolis, MN: Desiring God, 2012).
2. *The Holy Bible: English Standard Version* (Wheaton, IL: Crossway Bibles, 2016), Ex 3:5.
3. As quoted in Don J. Payne, *Already Sanctified: A Theology of the Christian Life in Light of God's Completed Work* (Grand Rapids, MI: Baker Publishing Group, 2020), 80, Kindle.
4. Wayne Grudem, *Systematic Theology: An Introduction to Biblical Doctrine*, Second Edition. (Grand Rapids, MI: Zondervan Academic, 2020), 934–935.

3. LUNCH BOX

1. These four points are from Kenneth O. Gangel, *John*, vol. 4, Holman New Testament Commentary (Nashville, TN: Broadman & Holman Publishers, 2000), 62.

5. BEAUTIFUL GLUE

1. Trevin Wax, *Rethink Your Self: The Power of Looking Up before Looking In*, (Nashville, TN: B&H Publishing Group, 2020), 1653, Kindle.

6. BACK IN WHACK

1. Billy Graham, "Billy Graham on What He Does Best," *Christianity Today* (Carol Stream, IL: Christianity Today, 1983), 28–31.
2. I don't recall the source of this quote, but Stonestreet's the president of the Colson Center for Christian Worldview…an insightful thinker and author.

7. AND WILLING

1. Source: https://www.cybersalt.org/pearly-gates-jokes/long-marriage
2. The summary of how the apostles weren't ready came from Eternal Impact's newsletter that cited "Joan Chittister in the book *Sacred Fire: A vision for Deeper Human & Christian Maturity by Ronald Rolheiser* (Image, 2014)."
3. John Steinbeck, *East of Eden*, as quoted by Jack Deere, *Even in Our Darkness: A Story of Beauty in a Broken Life* (Grand Rapids: Zondervan Publishing House, 2018), 276, Kindle.

10. ANGELS AND ORPHANS

1. One of the best scenes from one of the best movies *evah*. https://www.youtube.com/watch?v=KN9c2TAWMlg. And yes, I actually played this on the podcast. Because no Bible reading podcast is complete without the occasional Monty Python reference.
2. See also 1 Peter 4:9, 3 John 5–8.
3. See 1 Timothy 3:2; Titus 1:8.
4. David K. Huttar, "Hospitality," *Baker Encyclopedia of the Bible* (Grand Rapids, MI: Baker Book House, 1988), 1006.
5. Robin G. Branch and Marvin R. Wilson, "Widows & Orphans," *Dictionary of Daily Life in Biblical & Post-Biblical Antiquity* (Peabody, MA: Hendrickson Publishers, 2014–2016), 422–423.
6. John Koenig, "Hospitality," ed. David Noel Freedman, *The Anchor Yale Bible Dictionary* (New York: Doubleday, 1992), 301.

14. BREATHING TOGETHER

1. As quoted in Paul David Tripp's fabulous book, *Dangerous Calling: Confronting the Unique Challenges of Pastoral Ministry* (Wheaton, IL: Crossway, 2012).

19. WHAT TO ASK AN ATHIEST

1. See Time Magazine: https://time.com/5159848/do-religious-people-live-longer/
2. See Pew Research: https://www.pewresearch.org/fact-tank/2019/01/31/are-religious-people-happier-healthier-our-new-global-study-explores-this-question/

20. PLUMS

1. Yes, I said "bidness." Because it reminds me of a former business partner lost to cancer. He and I would sometimes break into lines from Eddie Murphy's *Beverly Hills Cop*…and there's a line in there in which he says "bidness." Remember, these reflections are from my podcast scripts and, well, this is just keepin' it real.

21. BOOKS

1. You might be tempted at this point to go, "Yeah, but copies of copies of copies and…". Trust me, that's been answered satisfactorily and, while not covering it here, give me a shout. I'll happily point you to resources that will challenge you to see that all those copies are actually *why* we can trust our contemporary English Bibles.

23. SURELY

1. "The Gift: The Journey of Johnny Cash," YouTube TV, accesses August 14, 2021, https://tv.youtube.com/watch/eslxbYj11Vo?vpp=2AEA& vp=0gEEEgIwBQ%3D%3D.

24. GHOSTS

1. Did you know that "evangelicalism" developed in the first half of the 20th century as a response to both fundamentalism and progressivism? As I once heard someone say (maybe John Stott?), the of fundamentalism was losing its grace; the failure of progressivism was losing its anchor. Evangelicals re-centered on the idea that Jesus wasn't truth *or* grace, wasn't 50% truth and 50% grace, he's 100% both. Obviously the word "evangelical" is now a big fat mess (as addressed in the "Words" reflection herein.

BOOK ROGER TO SPEAK TO YOUR AUDIENCE

Roger Courville is the Chief Aha! Guy with #ForTheHope Ministries based in Portland, Oregon, helping people fall in love with Jesus to reach the people in His world.

Growing up with the Christian heritage of two grandfathers who were pastors, family strife sent him deep into rebellion running from God at the age of 13. Ten years later he was living the life of a rock band musician and deeply immersed in philosophy and a search for meaning apart from God. Another ten years later Roger discovered Christian thinkers delivering reasoned, evidence-based answers to life's biggest questions found in the embodiment of Truth, Jesus of Nazareth.

Given this background and work as a multi-company entrepreneur, Roger developed a passion to study theology in order to help skeptics and spiritual seekers, especially in the context of make sense of the Bible for outside-the-church "normal life." He added a master's degree in Christian apologetics to his bachelor's degree in business, adding an intensive study at Oxford Centre for Christian Apologetics along the way.

Fast facts

- Working on his doctorate at Denver Seminary
- Serves on the leadership team at Follower of One, a support and equipping community marketplace missionaries

- Serves as the Head of Strategy for Virtual Venues, LLC, a team of producers for virtual events and webinars
- Holds the Certified Speaking Professional designation of National Speakers Association — the highest earned achievement in the association

Book Roger to speak

Having spoken all over the world on topics of business and communications, Roger's current focus is preaching, teaching, and training, both through his #ForTheHope Daily Audio Bible podcast, and to help people of all backgrounds and cultures engage with questions of faith and God such as

- What do calling, meaning, and purpose look like in a world of confusion?
- How do I "get in the game for Jesus" when I have a day job?
- What does it look like to be a Christian in a "many paths" world? Isn't the Christian faith unreasonable?
- What wisdom does the Bible hold for us today, particularly in the marketplace?
- How does the Christian worldview offer something unique in the pursuit of human flourishing?

To discuss having Roger deliver a keynote presentation or hands-on workshop for your organization (on site, online, or both), send an email to hello@forthehope.com with a little about

- you and your audience
- the topic you're interested in (doesn't have to be one listed above), and

- the event date and location.

Soli Deo Gloria

- facebook.com/forthehope
- twitter.com/rogercourville
- instagram.com/joinforthehope

Made in the USA
Monee, IL
23 December 2021

85808215R00095